施璐德亚洲有限公司 编

施璐德年鉴 2020

VISION DRIVEN LIFE

CNOOD 2008 TO 2020

CNOOD Yearbook
(2020)

目录

1
爱女池宸如唔
To My Dear Daughter Chi Chen
Dennis Chi

6
罗蓉女士、林焕先生证婚词
A speech at the wedding of Mrs. Loreen Luo and Mr. Huan Lin
Dennis Chi

8
以"福"结缘
Meeting People with Blessings

14
感 想
Reflections
Luis Camacho Cherp

18
为人父
Be Dad
Nicolas Kipreos Almallotis

20
新冠肺炎疫情将改变我们的生活和工作方式
COVID-19 Will Change Our Lives and Our Way of Working
Nicolas Kipreos Almallotis

25
我妻子的新冠肺炎疫情抗击经历
My Wife's Experience with the COVID-19
Nicolas Kipreos Almallotis

28
见证 CNOOD 的成长与茁壮
A Witness to the Growth and Expansion of CNOOD
Paul Chen

32
后疫情时代业务发展计划
Business Plan for Post-Pandemic
Amir Tafti

40
静女其姝
My Beloved Daughter
Andy Wei

42
新冠肺炎疫情给我们带来的教训
Lessons from the COVID-19 Pandemic
Patricia Yaber Tacchini

46
星光不问赶路人，时光不负有心人
The Stars Don't Ask the Travelers and Time Never Lets the Determined Down
Loreen Luo

54
正视自己的内心
Face up to Your Inner Self
Billy Gu

59
当下每一天
Living Every Day of My Life
Chris Lee

62
少说太难，说我可以
Say "It's hard" less and "I can" more
Heather Zhang

65
2021 随想
Random Thoughts in 2021
Danni Xu

68
从心出发
Start with the Heart
David Wang

71
感于心　践于行
Embrace Warmth and Put it into Practice
Iris Tong

75
感恩，再出发
Grateful and Starting off again
Johnson Shen

78
好久不见
It's been a long time
Louise Ju

86
巴拿马之行
A Trip to Panama
Richard Cheng

94
2020 年的"幸运"
The "Fortunes" in 2020
Tommy Chen

99
佛系 + 奋斗 = 理想
A Buddha Mind + Struggling = Ideal
William Qiu

103
无题
Untitled
Heron Tang

104
2020 塞拉利昂行
A Trip to Sierra Leone in 2020
Charles Lee

111
时代的浪潮与个人选择
The Tide of the Times and Personal Choice
Raven Song

116
因为有梦，所以远方
Head toward the Distance for the Pursuit of the Dream
Jodie Zhou

122
实习感想
Thoughts after My Internship
Yingyue Cui

125
实习感想
Thoughts after My Internship
Yulan Liang

爱女池宸如唔

To My Dear Daughter Chi Chen

■ Dennis Chi

很想你。

18岁的成人礼,我在想象你成为新娘子的场景,也在回首18年来,我们的相处,我们的得与失,我们的功与过。

在很多人的眼里,爸爸为人唾弃。因此,作为非成功人士,我的话仅为一家之言,供商榷,如一直以来的样子。

家国情怀,一定得有。回头四顾,你现在的生活环境,比爸爸当初强上太多太多。一方水土养一方人,更是千千万万国人努力奋斗的结晶。我从事外贸经年日久,感触尤深。从最初的不被待见、饱受鄙夷,到如今的平等相待、和睦共处、良性竞争,个中艰辛,甘苦自知。科学,没有国界,但科学家是有国界的。我们在国外的地位和处境,是与国家的强盛密不可分的,与千千万万的国人的努力紧密相连,休戚与共。周恩来总理的"为中华之崛起而读书",以前适用,现在依旧适用,将来更适用。有志不在年高,志当存高远,并为之终身奋斗。

谨慎择业。一般,人有3个10年:23岁到33岁、33岁到43岁、43岁到53岁。人生的黄金30年,每个10年都为下一个10年打基础。择业,以自己的兴趣为宜,以自己难以割舍的兴趣为最,能成事,成大事。最忌讳朝秦暮楚,三心二意,浅尝辄止。若如此,则事不就,业不成,年老华发,悔之晚矣。

情商逆商。要有高情商。情商,简而言之,设身处地想他人所想,急他人所急。高情商,在于后天的学习,在于有一颗感恩的心,待人以诚,待人以德。严以律己,宽以待人。也要有高逆商,这尤其重要。现代社会,条件优良,一个小孩,有6个人呵护,恶果之一是温室里的花朵,禁不起大自然的风霜雨雪,凄风苦雨,很容易夭折。动不动就跳楼,时不时想寻死。自然界哪有凄风苦雨,凄和苦都是个人的感受,风雨都是自然的，没有风雨，就没有色彩缤纷的世界。成长，是靠自己的努力的。别人帮自己，是情分，要懂得感恩，要懂得回报。很多人在帮爸爸，帮过爸爸，他们一起成就了爸爸，爸爸不能回报的，就学他们，帮助更多的其他人，回报社会，让社会更温暖，让明天更美好。别人不帮自己，是本分，没有必要记恨，可能是他们没有能力，可能是他们不方便，如此而已。刻苦学习，勤奋努力，成功随缘。努力足够了，时间自然会让成功发生。

坚定自信。什么时候，都要相信自己，并不是刚愎自用。多听别人的意见，他山之石，可以攻玉。三人行必有我师焉，三个臭皮匠顶个诸葛亮，此之谓也。做决定，三思而后行，忌首鼠两端，瞻前顾后，畏首畏尾。做事情，非常忌讳虎头蛇尾，既动摇军心，影响士气，又损伤信用，打击威信。实不足取，需谨记，切记。

谨交友，慎择夫。交努力上进的朋友，交心胸开阔的朋友。人非圣贤，孰能无过。水至清则无鱼，人至察则无友。宜待人以宽，律己以严。择夫方面，建议选择心胸宽广，努力上进之人，人品宜好，尤其要有爱心和孝心。非爱，不宜也；非孝，难处也。

小孩多，善教育。小孩要多有一些为宜。小孩的教育则以因材施教，鼓励为主，尤忌打骂、贬损。童年的记忆是深刻的，童年的影响是深远的，三岁看八十，七岁看终身。己所不欲，勿施于人。小孩是父母的镜子，你怎么做，他怎么学。和孩子谈问题，不宜在早上，毁一天；不宜在晚上，毁一晚。榜样的力量是无穷的，做好自己，自然会有优秀的小孩。对小孩，最长情的告白是陪伴，全心的陪伴。七岁之前的陪伴尤其重要，不可缺失，之后会慢慢减少。约十三岁生日的时候，他们会有自己的生活，讨厌并拒绝与你一起过生日。小孩的好奇心，永远不要打击，要鼓励和加强。永远不要对小孩发火，因为他们会记住。

看书看书，看好书。全球最聪明的人，在公元前 600 年到前 500 年。读史以明志。现在的故事都可以在历史中找到影子。现实是历史的重复。强力推荐《论语》，半部《论语》治天下；《道德经》，道家学派代表作；《心经》和《金刚经》，释家最重要的经典；《理想国》，西方哲学经典呈现；《黄帝内经》，中医传统经典；《鬼谷子》，纵横家巨著。

巾短情长，暂且住笔。望爱女池宸永远健康、开心。

　　致！

　　学安！

爸　勇海于缅甸

2020 年 6 月 21 日

How I miss you!

At your coming-of-age ceremony, I am imagining the day you get married and looking back at our days, gains and losses, merits and faults over the past 18 years.

Daddy is despised by many people. As an unsuccessful man, therefore, I only speak for your deliberation and reference as usual.

Always be patriotic. The living environment you have now is much much better than what I had. Each place has its own way of supporting its own inhabitants, and more importantly, it's the result of millions of Chinese people struggling and making unremitting efforts. Engaged in foreign trade over the years, I am well aware of how hard it is to achieve a transition from being disrespected and despised in the past to equal treatment, harmonious co-existence and benign competition in the international arena. Science has no national boundaries, but scientists do. Our position and status abroad are inextricably linked to the strength of our nation and to the efforts of millions of Chinese people. "Studying for the rise of China" proposed by Premier Zhou Enlai applies to China in the past as well as in the present, and more so in the future. A man's ambition does not depend on his age. We shall always have our ambitions and strive for them throughout our life.

Be prudent in job selection. Generally, we have three golden ten-year periods, from 23 to 33, from 33 to 43 and from 43 to 53. Each ten-year period is laying a foundation for the next. Job selection should be based on your own interests, and mostly preferably, the interest you can't give up. Only such a job can help you succeed and accomplish something. The worst things in job selection are frequent changes, half-heartedness and no hard work. You can never succeed in this way and will regret your choices at your old age.

Develop a high EQ and a high AQ. To put it simply, EQ is putting yourself in other people's shoes and addressing people's problems. A high EQ is reflected in gratefulness, sincerity and virtue. Be severe with yourself and lenient with others. A high AQ is particularly important. The material conditions in modern society are so favourable that a kid is taken care of by 6 people. One of the disastrous effects is that this flower grown in the greenhouse is too delicate to withstand the test of nature and may easily wither. Kids grown under such an environment are prone to commit suicide. There is no bitterness in nature. All bitterness comes from how we feel. The wind and rain in nature makes a colorful world. Growth depends on your own efforts. Assistance from others show their affection to you, for which you should be grateful and return. Many people have helped and are helping Daddy, and they have made who I am today. For those I can't return the favor, I will learn from them and help more people to give back to the society and make a warmer community and a better tomorrow. Others not offering assistance to you show their choice, for which you shall never hold a grudge. Perhaps it's beyond their capability or it's inconvenient for them to render help. Study hard, work hard, and let success come when the time is right. Only when you work hard enough will success come over time.

Be confident. Believe in yourself no matter when. It's not to be headstrong, but to be open to others' opinions. Jade can be polished by stones from other hills. You can always learn from your companions. Two heads are better than one. Always think before you make a decision. Don't be overcautious or indecisive. The worst thing in business is indecisiveness which will not only undermine the morale, but also damage your credit and authority. Always remember that it's inadvisable to be indecisive.

Be cautious in making friends and choosing your other half. Make friends with those who are striving and open-minded. To err is human. There is no fish in clear water, and those who have a watchful eye will have no friends. Be generous to others, but strict with yourself. In choosing your other half, you are advised to look for those who are open-minded, progressive, morally upright, and more importantly, caring and filial. Someone you don't love won't be a good match; someone who is not filial will be impossible to spend the rest of your life with.

Have several kids and be smart in educating them. It's advisable to have several of your kids. Teach them according to their aptitude. Encourages them most of the time. Never hit or belittle them. Childhood memories can exert a profound impact on the remaining periods of life. You can see how one will be at the age of 80 when he is 3 years old and see how one will achieve throughout his life when he is 7 years old. Do not do to others what you do not want done to yourself. Kids are a mirror to parents. They will act the way you do. Do not talk to the kids about their problems in the morning, otherwise you will ruin their whole day; do not talk to the kids about their problems in the evening, otherwise you will ruin their whole night. A good example has boundless power. Set a good example, and your kids will grow to be outstanding. For kids, the best confession of love is wholehearted companionship. Companionship before the age of 7 is particularly important and indispensable. Reduce your companionship gradually after that.

At an age of about 13, they will have their own live, and they will hate and refuse spending their birthday with you. Never discourage a kid's curiosity. Encourage them to be curious. Never lose your temper with a child as they will remember it.

Read books and read good books. The smartest men in the world lived in 600 to 500 BC. You can clear your mind by reading history. Modern stories can be found in history. Reality is a repetition of history. I highly recommend that you read the following masterpieces: *The Analects of Confucius* (a great book of management), *Tao Te Ching* (the representative work of Taoism), *Heart Sutra and Diamond Sutra* (the most important classic Buddhist works), *The Republic* (the classic work of western philosophy), *The Inner Canon of Huangdi* (traditional Chinese medicine work), and *Guiguzi* (the monumental work of political strategists).

This letter is too short to describe how much I love you. Wish you health and happiness forever.

Yours sincerely,

Happy study!

Daddy Dennis
Written in Myanmar on June 21, 2020

池勇海 / Dennis Chi

男，汉族，1970 年生于湖北省仙桃市。武汉理工大学管理学硕士，硕士生导师为刘国新教授；复旦大学经济学博士，博士生导师为洪远朋教授。2008 年创立施璐德亚洲有限公司，现担任施璐德亚洲有限公司董事长。

Male, ethnic Han, born in Xiantao, Hubei Province in 1970. He received his master's degree in management from Wuhan University of Technology, where he studied under Professor Liu Guoxin, and received his Ph.D. in economics from Fudan University, where he studied under Professor Hong Yuanpeng. Dennis is now Chairman of CNOOD Asia Limited, which he founded in 2008.

罗蓉女士、林焕先生证婚词

A speech at the wedding of Mrs. Loreen Luo and Mr. Huan Lin

■ Dennis Chi

各位来宾，女士们，先生们：

大家好！非常荣幸受罗蓉女士、林焕先生委托，致证婚词。我是施璐德亚洲有限公司董事长，他们俩的同事。

罗蓉女士，才女，敬师长，孝父母，友同事，为人谦，待人和，善致财，有担当。做媳妇，万里挑一；为人母，德行天下。教子必有方；育女必有章。娶此女，门楣光耀。

林焕先生，俊男，出可将，入能相，能隐忍，敢担待，为人谦，待人和，为灵地一人杰，是施璐德一台柱。有此男，家道绵长。

风云际会，人才辈出。时不我待，只争朝夕。祝比翼鸟振翅翱翔，愿连理枝根深叶茂。是为证。

Dear guests, ladies and gentlemen,

I am honored to speak to you at the wedding of Mrs. Loreen Luo and Mr. Huan Lin. I am the chairman of CNOOD and a coworker of the newly wedded.

Mrs. Loreen Luo is a talented woman who is respectful to her superiors, filial to her parents and friendly to her coworkers. Such a modest, amicable and responsible lady is a perfect choice for a daughter-in-law. She will be a virtuous mother who knows how to raise and educate children. She will bring honor to the family name.

Mr. Huan Lin is a handsome and outstanding man who is tolerant, responsible, modest and approachable. He is one pillar of CNOOD. He will sustain the family name.

Talented people come out in large numbers. Time and tide wait for no man. May you have a happy marriage!

施璐德亚洲有限公司董事长 池勇海
于 2020 年 12 月 5 日

Dennis Chi, Chairman of CNOOD
December 5, 2020

罗蓉女士、林焕先生证婚词

各位来宾，女士们，先生们：

大家好。非常荣幸受罗蓉女士、林焕先生委托致证婚词。我是施璐德亚洲有限公司董事长，他们俩的同事。

罗蓉女士，才女，敬师长，孝父母，友同事，为人谦，待人和，善致财，有担当。作媳妇，万里挑一；为人母，德行天下。教子必有方；育女必有章。娶此女，门楣光耀。

林焕先生，俊男，出可将，入能相，能隐忍，敢担待，为人谦，待人和，为天地一人杰，是施璐德一台柱。有此男，家道绵长。

风云际会，人才辈出。时不我待，只争朝夕。祝比翼鸟振翅翱翔，愿连理枝根深叶茂。

是为证。

施璐德亚洲有限公司
董事长：池勇海
于 2020 年 12 月 5 日

以"福"结缘

——施璐德合伙人丁征宇专访

Meeting People with Blessings

— An Exclusive Interview with Zhengyu Ding, a Partner of CNOOD

我觉得拜师不分年龄,能者居之。即使是比我年轻很多的人,如果我想向他学东西,我也会毫不犹豫地真诚拜师。

——丁征宇

小编:丁总,您每年新年都会很用心地利用自己休息的时间给公司的同事和一些朋友写"福"字,送祝福。您的初衷是什么呢?

丁征宇:对的,近几年农历新年前夕,我都会利用周末来书写"福"字,赠送给公司同事和一些平常工作、生活中有联系的好朋友。我的出发点很简单,新年嘛,送祝"福",让大家有个吉祥如意的新年,营造一个节日的气氛,祝愿朋友们来年福气满满,福星高照。同时,我也觉

I believe that what matters in mentorship is not age but ability. Even if it's someone who is much younger than me, I will accept such mentorship without hesitation if I want to learn something from them.

–Zhengyu Ding

Editor: Mr. Ding, you have been writing the Chinese character Fu (meaning Blessings) to our coworkers and friends in your spare time to send your regards before the Spring Festival every year. What made you start this tradition?

Mr. Ding: Yes, I have been doing it in the weekends when the Spring Festival is approaching in the past few years. I have sent it to our coworkers and good friends at work or in life. I had the simple idea of sending "blessings" to wish everyone an auspicious New Year and good luck in the

得这是中国传统文化的一种传承和传播形式，是我们文化自信的一种体现。许多外国的同事、朋友和客户，收到我的"福"字后都表示非常开心和喜欢。

小编：我们发现您给大家送的"福"字，字体非常多样，风格有庄重有俏皮。您习书法多少年了呢？是什么派系？

丁征宇：这次主要书写的"福"字为正楷、隶书、行楷、行草等。风格有庄严有俏皮，水平不怎么高，主要是图个热闹。我重新捡起习字也是近四年左右的事情，早期年少时习字临摹柳公权的玄秘塔、颜真卿的多宝塔，最近几年临摹赵孟頫的字。

最近四年，我都会在春节前花时间特地练习"福"字，有朋友曾经开玩笑说，老丁就只会写"福"字。其实，我在读小学时就喜欢练毛笔字，在中学就中断没练了。仅在中学时，曾担任校宣传委员，每周负责四块大的黑板报，结合当时时代背景，需要书写一些大幅标语。后来到上大学，紧接着工作后近40年的时间再也没接触过毛笔字了，说起来也是有点蛮可惜的。

upcoming year and to add festivity to the holiday. Meanwhile, I believe it's a way to carry forward and spread the traditional Chinese culture and a reflection of our cultural confidence. Many foreign coworkers, friends and customers are delighted to receive my Chinese character Fu.

Editor: We have noticed that you have written the Chinese character Fu in a variety of scripts and styles, solemn or smart. How many years have you practiced calligraphy? What's your calligraphy school?

Mr. Ding: The character Fu has been primarily written in regular script, official script, running-regular script and running-cursive script. The styles may be solemn or smart. They are not well written. I have been doing it for fun. It was about four years ago that I restarted calligraphy practicing. In my childhood, I practised calligraphy after Xuanmita of LIU Gongquan and Duobaota of YAN Zhenqing. It was not until the past several years that I started to imitate the calligraphy of ZHAO Mengfu.

Over the past four years, I have spent time practicing the character Fu before the Spring Festival. A friend of mine said jokingly that Fu was the only character that I knew how to write. As a matter of fact, I liked practicing with a brush in my primary school years until my middle school days. I worked as the commissary in charge of publicity in middle school and took charge of the four blackboard news. Back then I needed to write slogans on big banners. Later I went to college and then worked for

近几年来，因为交了不少书法圈的朋友，重新点燃了我练书法的兴趣和热情。经过这四年多的书写练习，已经有了一些进步。但是我内心还是十分渴望能够走上学书法的"正"路子，于是从2020年8月开启了正式学习书法之路，并有幸成为上海市宝山区书法家协会会员。我觉得人就是要活到老、学到老，即使再晚开始，我也认真对待。

2021年年初，我又拜沪上知名书法家为师，正式成为郑小云老师的入室弟子。郑小云师从韩天衡先生在书画印三项都有着非凡的造诣，并且取得了斐然的成绩。其实，郑小云老师与我同龄，但他从艺四十年有余，且十分刻苦，连韩天衡先生都说郑小云是他众多学生中学艺最勤奋、最出众者之一。在书法方面，郑小云绝对是我的师父，因此我就特地举办了一个很正式的拜师仪式，鹤发之年仍拜师。我觉得拜师不分年龄，能者居之。即使是比我年轻很多的人，如果我想向他学东西，我也会毫不犹豫地真诚拜师。

小编：您退休前主要从事什么工作，为什么钟情于书法？

about 40 years before I picked up brush calligraphy again. It's quite a pity.

As I have made quite a number of friends in the calligraphy circles in recent years, I have rekindled my interest and enthusiasm in practicing calligraphy. There has been some progress after more than four years of practice, yet I still yearn for studying calligraphy in school. Therefore, I started my formal calligraphy learning in August 2020, and I am honored to become a member of Shanghai Baoshan District Calligraphers Association. I believe that it's never too old to learn, and even if it is late to start something, I will take it seriously.

At the beginning of 2021, I became a student of ZHENG Xiaoyun, a famous calligrapher in Shanghai. Under the mentoring of Mr. HAN Tianheng, Mr. ZHENG has extraordinary attainments and achieves remarkable results in calligraphy, painting and seal-cutting. Though at the same age of me, Mr. ZHENG has been practicing art for more than forty years and works very hard. He is considered one of the most hard-working and brilliant students by Mr. HAN himself and is definitely my master in calligraphy. Therefore, I held a formal ceremony to take him as my teacher despite my old age. I believe that what matters in mentorship is not age but ability. Even if it's someone who is much younger than me, I will accept such mentorship without hesitation if I want to learn something from them.

Editor: What did you do before you retired? Why are you so keen on calligraphy?

丁征宇：退休前，我在世界五百强企业德国蒂森克虏伯工作，工作了近26年，主要从事钢铁冶金工业有关设备、原料进口以及各类钢管出口贸易等工作。书法是我的业余爱好，我觉得书法可以培养人的恬静性格，且能更深入了解中国文化，是提高自己的学识和素养的很好途径。书法能让人养成仔细、集中、冷静、持久的品质，不仅能磨炼意志力，同时能提高自身的审美能力等。

小编：您从蒂森克虏伯退休后，现在又继续在施璐德担任导师且几乎每天都来公司，您会不会觉得有些辛苦？退休了为什么还要继续工作，为什么选择加入施璐德？

丁征宇：今天是2021年2月8日，也是我退休后入职CNOOD整整7个月。经过这7个月与CNOOD的同事们相处，我感到十分高兴，没感到任何辛苦，也完全没有觉得自己是一位已经退休的前辈，和同事相处十分融洽，自己也很有热情和动力，很多时候还是我带着他们这帮小年轻玩呢！

早在十多年前，那时候CNOOD还没成立，我就已经结识了创始人池总。当时，我就觉得他这个人有点不一样，为人

Mr. Ding: Before my retirement, I worked for ThyssenKrupp, a Fortune 500 company in Germany, for nearly 26 years. I mainly engaged in the import of equipment and raw material and export of all kinds of steel pipes in the iron and steel metallurgical industry. Calligraphy has always been a hobby of mine. I believe calligraphy can develop tranquility, and it is a good way to gain a deeper understanding of Chinese culture and to improve knowledge and accomplishments. It can further develop attentiveness, concentration, calmness and persistence, temper the willpower and enhance aesthetic ability.

Editor: After your retirement from ThyssenKrupp, you have been working as a mentor in CNOOD. Do you feel a bit exhausted coming to the Company almost every day? Why do you continue to work after your retirement? Why do you choose to join CNOOD?

Mr. Ding: It's February 8, 2021 today, which also marks my 7th month anniversary in CNOOD after my retirement. I am delighted to have worked with my coworkers in CNOOD for the past 7 months, and have no feeling of exhaustion at all. I have never thought of myself as a retired predecessor. I get along well with my coworkers. I am passionate and driven, and I have been organizing entertainment activities for the young people most of the time!

I met Mr. CHI, founder of CNOOD about ten years ago before its establishment. At that time, I felt that he is quite different

特别谦和，很有自己的见解，也有心胸和胆识，后来他创立 CNOOD 后我也一直关注着。这十几年来，也一直保持着良好的朋友关系，直到 2020 年 5 月我退休，池总就马上联系我，真诚地邀请我加入 CNOOD。

正式加入 CNOOD 后，我对 CNOOD 有了更深入的了解和体会，公司倡导的"共创、共治、共享""互相关心，创造开心"的理念和价值观深入人心。公司就像一个大家庭，每个员工每天都在成长中，即使像我这样退休返聘的人，也感觉每天都有新的进步。CNOOD 的员工都很优秀，自己的专业各有所长，是一支生机勃勃、老中青结合的精英团队。对我来说，在 CNOOD 也能有机会发挥多年来在此行业内积累的经验的优势。与现公司的同仁们并肩奋斗，自己真的感觉工作一天反而年轻一天，真的在践行"活到老，学到老"。

小编：作为施璐德特聘导师，您觉得您在哪些方面是可以利用自己的丰富经验帮助施璐德进行提高和完善的？对施璐德的学生们又有哪些要求和期待呢？

丁征宇：自己作为 CNOOD 的特聘导师，在 CNOOD 这个成熟而又有活力的大家庭中，利用自己多年在行业里的严谨工作态度和丰富的经验，与 CNOOD 年轻团

from others. He is very modest and has his own ideas, broad-minded and bold. Later he founded CNOOD, and I had kept my eyes on it. For the past decade, we have maintained a good friendship. When I retired in May 2020, Mr. CHI immediately called me and sincerely invited me to join CNOOD.

After my entry into CNOOD, I have developed a deeper understanding of the company. The ideas of "co-creation, co-governance and sharing," and values of "care for each other and create happiness" have been internalized by everyone of us. The company is like a big family where every employee grows every day. Even for people like me who are rehired after retirement, we still feel like making new progress every day. All employees of CNOOD are brilliant and have their own expertise. It's a vibrant elite team of young, middle-aged and senior members. For me, I really feel younger every day I work with the coworkers shoulder by shoulder and give play to what's learned in the industry over the years. It's really "never too old to learn" for me.

Editor: As a specially-appointed mentor of CNOOD, in what areas do you think you can use your rich experience to help CNOOD improve? What are your requirements and expectations for the students in CNOOD?

Mr. Ding: As a specially-appointed mentor of CNOOD, I make use of my rigorous work attitude and rich experience in the industry to exchange with the

队多交流，相互学习，共同提高，共同成长。为不断创新，不断进取，不断开拓的 CNOOD 大家庭再创佳绩。不忘初心，砥砺前行，贡献自己的微薄之力。

小编：丁总，感谢您的时间和耐心的回答，通过您的回答我们才真正地了解到您的"福"缘和学习精神。我们的专访马上就要接近尾声了，您再给我们说点什么吧？

丁征宇：不多说了，不多说了，今天话太多了呢（笑，害羞并摆手）。我就以一首打油诗结尾吧，纯属热闹，大家凑合看。

以福结缘多助得，
余热生辉晚年乐。
再创三春奋斗者，
宏图大展施璐德。

young team of CNOOD for the purpose of mutual learning, common improvement and growth in the well-established and vibrant big family of CNOOD. I do my bit as we stay true to our mission and forge ahead for greater achievements of the innovating, progressive and pioneering CNOOD.

Editor: Thank you for your time and patience, Mr. Ding. You have shed light on your persistence of making friends through Fu calligraphy and learning spirit. As our interview is drawing to a close, would you like to say something more?

Mr. Ding: That's all for what I can say. I have been talking too much (smiling, shy and waving his hand). I would like to end this interview with doggerel. It's just for fun.

Make friends and receive help through Fu calligraphy;

Enjoy a happy late life based on previous experience;

May all strivers gain what they work for;

May CNOOD embrace great success.

丁征宇
Zhengyu Ding

1960 年 5 月出生，浙江绍兴人，毕业于上海应用技术大学冶金工程专业。1994—2020 年就职于德国蒂森克虏伯公司，2020 年 5 月退休；同年 7 月加入施璐德亚洲有限公司。工作认真、做事靠谱，正直善良、热爱生活，乐于助人、善于交友，喜欢书法和运动。

Born in May 1960 in Shaoxing City in Zhejiang Province, Ding Zhengyu graduated from Shanghai Institute of Technology majoring in metallurgical engineering. He worked in Thyssenkrupp from 1994 to 2020 and retired in May 2020. In the same year, he joined CNOOD Asia Limited. He always works seriously with great reliability. Integrity and kindness are the essence of his personality. He attaches great importance to enjoying life and is always ready to help others and good at making friends. He is fond of calligraphy and sports.

感 想

Reflections

■ Luis Camacho Cherp

如果把生活看作一列正在行驶的火车，时而高速行进，时而低速向前，时而短暂停站，那么所有这些因素都会不经意地或经意地干扰你的生活，因你的前进方向和目的地的不同而不同；这列火车汇聚着各种故事、上下车的各色乘客、迎来送往、旅途中的陪伴、回忆、感情，但最重要的是感情。

父亲一年半前去世了，但我一直记得他在我孩童时期一直反复强调的一件事："人们会忘记你所说的话，大部分人忘记你所做之事，但他们永远不会忘记的是你给他们的感受，所以你要尽你所能让人心情愉快。"

这条忠告再加上我母亲的榜样塑造了我的待人处世之道，因为母亲总是热情四射、心情愉快、给人以舒服的感觉。这种待人处世之道与竞争激烈的职业生涯的交织让一切变得复杂起来，让我倍感失

If I see life as a moving train, high speed on some occasions, slower routes, short stops, all factors that intervene in your life casually or not, by your training, by destination; everything comes together in this train, experiences, people who get on and off the train, welcomes, farewells, accompaniment during the journey, memories, feelings, above all feelings.

My father passed away a year and a half ago, I always remember something that he repeated to me on some occasions since I was a child: "People forget what you say, most people forget what you do, but what they never ever forget is how you make them feel, so make people feel good whenever you can."

This advice, together with the example of my mother, always welcoming, cheerful, comfortable, has conditioned my way of acting in life, this way of proceeding is complicated to combine

望、备受挫折，但我不断学习，不断思考母亲会如何做，因为她总是面带微笑，特别是眼睛里会闪着亮光，唱出著名歌手荷西·德雷克斯勒的歌词：

"每个人都给予，一个人得到什么取决于他给予什么，没有比这更简单的道理，没有别的规则，没有什么会失去，一切都会转化。"

在加入施璐德这个大家庭的几个月里，我终于弄清楚见到 Dennis 时的第一感觉，当时我并不知道他是谁或他的职位是什么，当然他也不知道我是谁。这是一次真诚的会面，我们都获邀参加一项活动，相伴一个星期，他让人心情愉悦，一切都无关专业或商业利益。一段时间之后，我仍然有这种感觉。如今加入施璐德这个大家庭，我们之间会涉及专业或商业利益，但是依然时刻维持着那种教育、陪伴、支持和善意精神。

with a competitive professional life. It has cost me many disappointments and frustrations, learning, always thinking about how my mother would act, with a smile on her mouth and especially in her eyes, applying the words of the famous Jorge Drexler song:

"Each one gives what he receives, then receives what he gives. Nothing is simpler; there is no other rule: nothing is lost; everything is transformed."

In the last months as a member of CNOOD, I have been able to verify the first sensation I experienced when meeting Dennis without knowing who he was or what he did or he who I was. It was a sincere meeting, with good feelings, based on the accompaniment for a week in an event in which we were both invited, without professional or commercial interests. Some time later I still have this feeling, but now as a member of the CNOOD family, now with professional and business interests, but maintaining that spirit of education, accompaniment, support and kindness at all times.

将一个理念应用到一个高水平超专业公司，我当时并不认为这种结合可能付诸实践。

由于个人培训和职业生涯的原因，在日常工作中，我总是将创意放在第一位，而将技术培训放在次要位置。现在我必须感谢施璐德，让我学会在工作流程中实现这两个方面的平衡。

我很高兴能够得到个人的成长，学习到新技能，同时为施璐德的持续发展贡献自己的一份力量。

我的目的是推广中国和西班牙这两种相差甚远的文化方式，丰富彼此，取长补短，共同成长，实现共赢。

最后，我想引用父亲的另一句话："不要投资于物质主义，只要可以都要投资于感觉。"

A philosophy applied to a high level super professional company, I really did not think this combination was possible.

Due to my training and professional life, in my daily work, creativity has always prevailed over the technical training received; now I must thank and learn from CNOOD to balance these two aspects in my work procedures.

I am excited to grow as a person and develop new skills while contributing my bit in the continued development of CNOOD.

My intention is to promote the cultural approach of two ways being so distant, China and Spain, enriching each other, taking the best of each part to continue growing together and experiencing the best sensations.

I end with another phrase from my father: "Do not invest in materialism, invest whenever you can in sensations."

▶ 原文（西班牙语）

Si observo la vida como un tren en marcha, alta velocidad en algunas ocasiones, recorridos más lentos, paradas cortas, todos los factores que interviene en tu vida por casualidad o no, por tu preparación, por el destino; todo se une en este tren, experiencias, personas que suben y bajan del tren, bienvenidas, despedidas, acompañamiento durante el trayecto, recuerdos, sensaciones, ante todo sensaciones.

Mi padre falleció hace año y medio, siempre recuerdo algo que me repitió en algunas ocasiones desde que yo era niño: "La gente olvida lo que dices, la mayoría de la gente olvida lo que haces, pero lo que nunca jamás olvida es como les haces sentir, por ello haz sentir bien a la gente siempre que puedas."

Este consejo, junto con el ejemplo de mi madre, siempre acogedora, alegre, confortable, han marcado mi manera de actuar en la vida, esta forma de proceder es complicada combinarla con la vida profesional tan competitiva, me ha costado muchas desilusiones, frustraciones, aprendizajes, siempre pensando en cómo actuaría mi madre, con una sonrisa en la boca y sobre todo en los ojos, aplicando la letra de la famosa canción de Jorge Drexler :

"Cada uno da, lo que recibe, luego recibe lo que da, nada es más simple, no hay otra norma: nada se pierde, todo se transforma."

En los últimos meses como miembro de CNOOD, he podido comprobar la que la primera sensación que experimenté al conocer a Dennis sin saber yo quien era ni a que se dedicaba ni él quien era yo tampoco, fue un encuentro sincero, de buenas sensaciones, basado en el acompañamiento durante una semana en un evento en el que estábamos invitados los dos, sin intereses profesionales ni comerciales. Tiempo después sigo teniendo esta sensación, pero ahora como miembro de la familia CNOOD, ahora ya con intereses profesionales y empresariales, pero manteniendo ese espíritu de educación, acompañamiento, apoyo y amabilidad en todo momento.

Una filosofía aplicada a una empresa superprofesional de alto nivel, realmente no pensaba que fuera posible esta combinación.

Debido a mi formación y vida profesional, en mi trabajo diario siempre ha primado la creatividad ante la formación técnica también recibida, ahora debo agradecer y aprender de CNOOD para equilibrar esos dos aspectos en mis procedimientos de trabajo.

Estoy ilusionado de poder crecer como persona y desarrollar nuevas capacidades mientras aporto mi granito de arena en el continuo desarrollo de CNOOD.

Mi intención es fomentar el acercamiento cultural de dos formas de ser tan distantes, China y España, enriqueciendo una a la otra, tomando lo mejor de cada parte para seguir creciendo juntas y experimentando las mejores sensaciones.

Acabo con otra frase de mi padre: "no inviertas en materialismo, invierte siempre que puedas en sensaciones."

Luis Camacho Cherp

已婚，有两个女儿和一个儿子，喜欢旅行、阅读、家庭生活、乡村生活、烹饪、音乐、运动，认为最重要的是和朋友聚会。

Married, with two daughters and a son, he enjoys traveling, reading, family life, the countryside, cooking, music, sports and above all meetings with friends.

为人父

Be Dad

■ Nicolas Kipreos Almallotis

  为人父是一段没有地图的道路，一条可以改变你且没有回头路可走的道路，意味着开启了一场肯定会改变自己生活的冒险，更标志着一个孩子诞生的神奇起点。简而言之，为人父是一份只有当你怀抱孩子时才能理解的礼物，你可以体会到永不重复的惊喜，无法言表的美好。

  为人父既要当一名教师，又要当一名学生，边教边学。这是一所人生大学，多余的东西会被遗忘，而且这个世界太小，装不下你所创造的奇迹。因为这个原因，为人父是无条件的降服，你的余生将会受到限制，还会有牺牲、激情和爱。

  为人父是感受脆弱、害怕，并确定任何障碍都不重要，因为你别无选择，只能克服。在那一刻，你会发现你可以处理任何事情，因为孩子是最好的礼物，所以你

  Being a father is the path that has no map, the path of no return that transforms you, the adventure that you know for sure will change your life, the magical starting point of bringing children into existence. Being a father is, in short, a personal gift that you can only understand when you have a child in your arms, surprising for the unrepeatable, fascinating for the indescribable.

  Being a father is being a teacher and a student at the same time, learning by teaching, is enrolling in the university of life, where the superfluous is forgotten and the world that is too small for you with the wonder you created. For this reason, being a father is the unconditional surrender that conditions the rest of your life, filling it with sacrifice, passion and love.

  Being a parent is feeling vulnerable, being afraid, and confirming that the obstacle no longer matters because you have no choice but to do well, and at that moment

将会为之付出一切。

为人父就是不管失去什么都倾其所有，因为最后赢的是你。为人父就是全力以赴，做到最好！

you discover that you can handle everything that comes along because your children are the best thing that has happened to you and so you will do anything.

Being a father is giving everything no matter what you lose, because you always win. Being a father is giving your best!

Nicolas Kipreos Almallotis

尼古拉斯出生于一个希腊裔家庭，当初他们为谋求更好机遇而举家徙居智利时，可谓身无长物，唯有成功之渴望、自由之身心，以及他们的爱心和对天主计划的信德。此后，他与兄弟和两个姐妹在极为清晰的原则指引下长大成人，受到过良好的教育和道德的熏陶，养成了简朴的生活方式，心中充满无尽之爱。几家声誉卓著的机构培养陶冶了他，帮助他实现远大理想。1993年，他与帕特里夏结为伉俪，育有四个儿女（玛丽亚·赫苏斯、比森特、本哈明、华金），一家人其乐融融。他信仰虔诚，日进日新，对待同事，真诚友善，但对自己认定正确之事抑或更佳之策，则必为之争辩，不轻言放弃。恒守敬人之道，临事唯以信、爱、真。一以贯之者，宽以待人、严以求实。

他不怕犯错，但若因自己未做分内之事、未能恪尽职守而累及他人，则必心怀畏惧。在施璐德，他受到热情欢迎，颇感自在裕如。自觉有义务为公司服务，期待不久即可回报。

他的座右铭是："正面思考，积极主动，充满自信，信仰坚定，生活必将更为稳定，更多实干行动，留下更丰富的经历和成果。"

Nicolas was born to a Greek family who moved to Chile looking for better opportunities. They brought with them nothing but their desire to succeed, their mental and physical freedom, their love and their faith in God's designs. Thus, he was raised with his brother and two sisters with very clear principles, good education and morals, simplicity in the way of living and infinite love. He was molded in several institutions of great reputation that have allowed him to reach great ideals. He married Patricia in 1993 and has four children (Maria Jesus, Vicente, Benjamin and Joaquin), forming a happy family. He lives his faith piously, tries to improve every day and is honest and kind to his colleagues, but he also always defends what he believes to be right or better, never giving up easily. He always treats people with respect and deals with affairs with integrity, love and sincerity. He is always soft on the person and hard on the issue.

He is not afraid of making mistakes, but he feels ashamed if others are affected because he didn't fulfill his responsibilities. He feels very comfortable at CNOOD where he has been generously welcomed. He feels a debt to the company and hopes to pay it off soon.

His maxim is "think positively and actively, with confidence and faith, and life will become more secure, more fraught with actions and richer in experience and achievement."

新冠肺炎疫情将改变我们的生活和工作方式
COVID-19 Will Change Our Lives and Our Way of Working

■ Nicolas Kipreos Almallotis

在法国小说《鼠疫》里，阿尔贝·加缪问痛苦是否可以不施加于个人，而是由大众共同承受。他写道，危机颠覆了现有的社会秩序，并造成了范式转变。新冠肺炎疫情影响社会方方面面，影响可持续发展的各个维度。这种范式转变让所有人都看到了系统的内在联系，打破了部门、机构甚至国家的界限。在各国政府首次实施封国措施以遏制病毒传播近一年来，越来越多的人认为，未来将有更多员工被远程雇佣，居家办公。

这些发展趋势也将产生长期影响。到目前为止，我们的工作、教育和社交逐渐进入数字时代，而这种转变已经出现了加速趋势，并可能改变与我们息息相关的方方面面，如我们工作、学习和参与的方式。新冠肺炎疫情持续的时间越长，新的

In the French novel *The Plague*, Albert Camus asks if suffering can exist not in individuals but as a shared public experience. Crisis, he writes, upends existing social order and creates paradigm shifts. COVID-19 affects all aspects of society and all dimensions of sustainable development. This paradigm shift exposes systemic inter-connectedness for everyone to see and breaks boundaries — sectoral, institutional or even national. Nearly a year after governments first imposed lockdowns to contain the virus, there is a growing consensus that in the future more staff will be hired remotely and work from home.

These developments will also have long-term implications. The so far gradual move of our work, education and socialization into the digital space is already seeing a major acceleration and may change core aspects of our identities

生活方式越容易出现，最终影响公共建筑和空间、图书馆、大学与中小学的使用。虽然数字化普及率已经很高，许多公共服务越来越多地实现了在线提供，但新冠肺炎疫情将加快数字化转型的速度，而不仅仅是优化我们的社会。信任和可追溯性的作用可能会提升：特别是食品和药品的更短和可追溯的价值链；作为一种去中心化、更快的生产形式的3D打印和无现金经济的扩张可能会越来越受欢迎（就像现在的中国一样）。

新冠病毒不歧视任何人。每个人都可能受到影响，不论阶级、种族或国籍。然而，医疗保健和隔离或感染，目前取决于所在地、财富多少、是否有保护措施，在

as well as how we work, learn and engage. The longer the pandemic continues, the more new ways of operating will emerge, ultimately influencing the use of public buildings and spaces, libraries, universities and schools. While the digital uptake is already high with many public services increasingly provided online, the pandemic will accelerate the speed at which digital transformation as well as optimization of our societies takes place. The role of trust and traceability is likely to increase: shorter and traceable value-chains, especially for food and medicines; the expansion of 3D printing, as a form of decentralized and faster production, and cashless economies may gain traction (like in China now-days).

Pandemics do not discriminate. Everyone can be affected regardless of class, race or nationality. However, healthcare and the experience of being

某些情况下，还取决于年龄。新冠肺炎疫情引发了新一轮的种族主义、仇外主义和孤立主义。这一新的现实将推动新的社会保障形式的诞生，同时也将提高人们对建立更强大的公共部门的期望。

工作场所仅仅是员工在正常办公时间占用的物理空间的日子已经一去不复返了。当前的新冠肺炎疫情已经模糊了实体办公室和实际工作场所之间的界限。工作场所实现了真正的数字化；员工正在以前所未有的方式进行沟通和协作。通过整合员工使用的技术（从电子邮件、即时通信到虚拟会议），数字工作场所打破了沟通障碍，使大家能够通过促进效率、创新和增长来改变员工体验。

2020—2021年，新冠肺炎疫情使全球劳动力市场陷于混乱之中。其短期后果是突然而严重的：数百万人被迫休假或失业，其他人随着办公室关闭而迅速适应了在家工作模式。像在医院和杂货店、垃圾车和仓库的许多工作，需要工作人员现场办工但他们均遵守了减少新型冠状病毒传播的新规定。

新冠肺炎疫情首次提高了实际工作

isolated or sick is, right now, dependent on location, wealth, protections and in some cases, age. The pandemic has sparked new waves of racism, xenophobia and isolationism. This new reality will push for the creation of new forms of social protection, with also an expectation for a stronger public sector.

Gone are the days when the workplace was merely a physical space employees occupied during regular office hours. Today's COVID-19 situation has faded the lines between the physical office and the place where work actually happens. The workplace becomes truly digital; employees are communicating and collaborating in unprecedented ways. By integrating the technologies that employees use (from e-mail, instant messaging to virtual meeting), the digital workplace breaks down communication barriers, positioning you to transform the employee experience by fostering efficiency, innovation and growth.

The COVID-19 pandemic disrupted labor markets globally during 2020 and 2021. The short-term consequences were sudden and severe: millions of people were furloughed or lost jobs, and others rapidly adjusted to working from home as offices closed. Many other workers were deemed essential and continued to work in hospitals and grocery stores, on garbage trucks and in warehouses, yet under new protocols to reduce the spread of the novel coronavirus.

For the first time, COVID-19 has

方面的重要性，施璐德更是一直如此。疫情促使众多企业迅速采取可能会持续执行的新举措。新冠肺炎疫情对劳动力最明显的影响可能是远程工作员工数量的急剧增加。一些公司在疫情期间实行远程办公并获得成功经验后，已经计划使用灵活的工作空间，此举将减少公司所需的整体空间，并减少每天进入办公室的员工数量。

远程办公也可能影响工作会议的形式，因为在疫情期间，视频会议的广泛使用使人们慢慢地接受了虚拟会议，并取得了良好的结果，降低了从一个地方转移到另一个地方的时间成本。

许多消费者在疫情期间发现了电子商务和其他在线活动的便利性。2020—2021年，全球电子商务规模的增长速度是新冠肺炎疫情暴发前的五倍。大约有四分之三在疫情期间首次使用数字渠道的用户表示，当一切恢复"正常"后，他们将继续使用这些渠道。

远程医疗、网上银行和流媒体娱乐等其他类型的虚拟交易也在快速发展。在四个月里，全球在线医生咨询量增长了十倍以上。随着经济的重新开放，这些在线业务量可能会有所下降，但很可能继续远高于疫情暴发之前的水平。

elevated the importance of the physical dimension of work, and we have been living it in the CNOOD organization. The pandemic pushed companies to rapidly adopt new behaviors that are likely to stick. Perhaps the most obvious impact of COVID-19 on the labor force is the dramatic increase in employees working remotely. Some companies are already planning to shift to flexible workspaces after positive experiences with remote work during the pandemic, a move that will reduce the overall space they need and bring fewer workers into offices each day.

Remote work may also put a dent at work-place meetings, as the extensive use of videoconferencing during the pandemic has ushered in a new acceptance of virtual meetings with excellent results, losing less time in moving from one place to another.

Many consumers discovered the convenience of e-commerce and other online activities during the pandemic. In 2020 – 2021, the share of e-commerce grew five times the rate worldwide before COVID-19. Roughly, three-quarters of people using digital channels for the first time during the pandemic say they will continue using them when things return to "normal".

Other kinds of virtual transactions such as telemedicine, online banking and streaming entertainment have also taken off. Online doctor consultations grew more than tenfold in the last four months in the world. These virtual practices may decline somewhat as economies reopen

新冠肺炎疫情已经造成了毁灭性的长期危机,它很可能会引发连锁效应——这要求我们重新定义长期以来的偏好,以支持缓解、适应和恢复力的新模式。如果这场危机真的走上了预期的道路,这将带来结构性的和深远的影响,我们已知的和经过验证的恢复模式可能不会奏效。国际组织已经下调了增长预测,全球股市也在下跌。只有地球的呼吸变得更好了。

这次新冠肺炎疫情以创纪录的时间在全球范围内产生了冲击波。要确保这些结构性转变不会加剧不平等和不公平态势,就需要动态管理、信息和学习的持续流动以及协作。它能够,也应该促成一种向更多、更好的以及毫无争议、协调的国际合作转变,正如它正在推动与中国政府合作那样,而不是我们现在看到的孤立主义。各生产环节需要转变思维和态度,这是《2030年议程》和《可持续发展目标》所呼吁的,但迄今收效甚微。

最后引用加缪的话来结束这篇文章,"我们在瘟疫时代学到的是:人身上值得赞美的东西比受到鄙视的多。"

but are likely to continue well above levels seen before the pandemic.

Devastating, as it is already now, the prolonged crisis produced by COVID-19 is likely to induce cascading effects — requiring us to recode our long-held preferences in favor of new models of mitigation, adaptation and resilience. If this crisis does take the expected pathway, implications will be structural and profound, and our known and tested recovery models may not work. The international organisms have downgraded their growth forecasts and global stock markets are falling. Only the planet is breathing better.

This pandemic has sent shockwaves across the globe in record time. Ensuring that these structural shifts do not exacerbate inequalities and inequity will require dynamic management, a continuous flow of information and learning, and collaboration. It can — and should — produce a shift towards more and better international cooperation — as it is promoting the cooperation with the Chinese government — and uncontested coordination, rather than the isolationism we see now. It could produce a shift of mindsets and attitudes at all levels, for which the Agenda 2030 and Sustainable Development Goals have called for with little success, at least until now.

To return to Camus: "What we learn in time of pestilence: that there are more things to admire in men than to despise."

我妻子的新冠肺炎疫情抗击经历

My Wife's Experience with the COVID-19

■ Nicolas Kipreos Almallotis

我的妻子是一名儿科医生，有着丰富的急诊经验，曾经治疗过感染新冠肺炎病毒的成年患者。这次新冠肺炎疫情抗击经历给她留下深刻印象，这就是我为什么想采访她，了解她的想法并将其分享给施璐德大家庭的原因。

亲爱的帕蒂，这次经历的什么给你最深刻的印象？

在治疗新冠肺炎患者中让我印象最深刻的是治疗过程让人痛心和残酷。病人不允许有探视者，那些在重症监护室插管和注射镇静剂的病人不能和医护人员交流。

医生和病人的关系如何？

作为一名医生，我只知道他的名字和相关的医学指标。在平常的疾病治疗中，我们对病人有更多的了解，可以通过家人和朋友的探访了解个人和人性方面更多的

My wife is a pediatrician, with great experience in emergency cases, and she as a doctor had to treat adult patients with COVID-19. Her experience was very strong and that is why I wanted to interview her to find out her thinking and share it with the CNOOD Family.

Dear Paty, what thing struck you the most of your experience?

The thing that truck me the most, from the experience of treating COVID-19 patients, was how heartbreakingly dehumanizing it was. Patients were not allowed to have visitors, and those intubated and sedated in the ICUs could not talk to you.

What was the relation with the patients?

As a doctor, I only knew a name and the medical parameters associated with the individual. During usual times, we get to know a little more about the patients —

信息。但在新冠肺炎治疗中，我们看到病人孤独地死去，没有家人陪伴，实在让人心碎。

采取各种保护措施也让你很难和病人沟通，对吧？

是的，因为戴上防护设备和口罩，我们会感觉与病人之间的沟通存在某种障碍。坦率地说，因为医院里的每个人都戴着口罩，甚至包括你认识的人和同事，这都是不人道的做法，彼此甚至不能会心一笑。

有哪些困难呢？

每个人都很迫切地想要做点什么来帮助病人。但现状让人疯狂和令人沮丧，每个人都充满强烈的绝望感。随着事态有所缓和，现在有更多的时间来评估已收集的大量数据，以便更好地评估哪些干预措施实际上是有效的，但仍有很多工作要做，我们仍有很多东西要学习。我们仍在想方设法地抗击这可怕的疫情。

当时资源缺乏，你们是怎么做的？

为了容纳汹涌而入的患者，我们的重症监护病房，甚至是儿科病房，都被改为成人新冠肺炎患者重症监护病房。我们采取了很多实用措施，以适应我们所处的环境。这并不容易。很多时候，我们不得不做出艰难的决定。很多医护人员在非常紧

the personal and human side, with families and friends visiting — but with COVID-19, it was heartbreaking to see people dying alone, without their families close to them.

Protecting yourself so much also made it difficult to connect with the patient, didn't it?

Yes, because wearing protective equipment and facemasks, we feel like there is another kind of barrier between our patients and us. Quite frankly, because everyone is wearing a mask in the hospital, even that's dehumanizing among the people you know and your colleagues — you can't even exchange a smile.

What was challenging?

That everyone was so desperate to do something, to try anything to help the patients. It was crazy and frustrating, but everyone felt this acute sense of desperation. As things have calmed down a bit, there is now more time to evaluate a lot of data that has been collected to better assess what interventions are actually effective, but there is still a lot of work to do and we still have a lot to learn. We are still in the midst of this terrible pandemic.

Since there was a lack of resources, how did you do it?

To accommodate the influx, our intensive care units, even the pediatric ones, were converted to adult COVID-19 intensive care units. We accommodated ourselves with a lot of pragmatism to the reality we were living in. It was not

张的环境下长时间工作,我们要抗击一种大家都不太了解的疾病。在很多情况下,我们的工作超出了本身的专业领域,但我们依然以积极的态度来工作,这是令人瞩目和让人温暖的。

最大的收获是什么?

可能是因为新冠肺炎疫情在一定程度上凸显了我们医疗体系和社会结构中各种本质上的不平等状况。并不是说我们平时不知道这些不平等状况,但在我的一生中,从来没有什么事情让这些不平等状况变得如此不可忽视。

easy. Many times, we had to make tough decisions. The number of people who worked extraordinary hours under very stressful circumstances, dealing with a disease that nobody understood very well, in many cases operating outside of their area of domain expertise, and did it with a positive attitude, was remarkable and heartwarming.

What was the biggest takeaway?

Probably the degree to which the pandemic highlighted all sorts of fundamental inequities in our healthcare system and our social structure. Not that one is not aware of them, but there has not ever been anything in my lifetime that has made it this impossible to ignore.

见证 CNOOD 的成长与茁壮

A Witness to the Growth and Expansion of CNOOD

■ Paul Chen

时光飞逝，转眼间从 2016 年的夏天在美国福陆工程公司退休后收到 CNOOD 董事长 Dennis 的邀请至今，已有 5 年。

在四十多年从事工程业的生涯（从台湾中鼎工程公司 CTCI 的 25 年到美国福陆工程公司 Fluor 的近 15 年，再到进入施璐德亚洲有限公司 CNOOD 的 5 年），我很幸运地能在这三家公司中，学到不少专业知识，得到工作能力的培养以及国际视野的建立。回忆过往，个人的职业生涯历历在目。

首先在 CTCI（主要以石油化工、电站、公共工程的设计、采购、建造总承包为主），除了前三年在管道设计部工作，之后的 22 年则参与公司的国内外工程，工作涉及采购、分包、物流以及商务，分别被派驻到沙特工作 2 年，派驻到美国工作 1 年，并负责 CTCI 在中国的工程项目

How time flies. It has been 5 years since I received the invitation from Chairman Dennis Chi to join CNOOD soon after I retired from Fluor Corporation in the summer of 2016.

Having worked in the engineering industry for more than forty years (25 years in CTCI, about 15 years in Fluor Corporation and 5 years in CNOOD), I have been fortunate to learn plenty of specialized knowledge from the three companies and develop my working competence and an international vision. Looking back, I feel like that my career only started yesterday.

During my service for CTCI (mainly engaged in EPC projects of petrochemicals, power plants and public works), I worked in the Pipeline Design Department in the first three years and then participated in the procurement, outsourcing, logistics and commercial operations of projects at

的采购及分包。由于工作的需要，一直循环出差于中东、亚洲、欧美各国家，因此增加了不少和国际人士的接触与相处的机会，更了解了如何去完成总承包项目。

2002年初我加入Fluor中国，负责其采购管理、合同管理及中国供应商的开发和管理。在这期间除了仍然从事石油化工、电站、公共工程建造工作外，还涉及矿业、纸业、医药、海上钻油工程及模块制造的工作。为了配合Fluor在全球的工程需要，我参与降低建造成本的工作。依Fluor的政策需求，我开发了各类中国的供应商、承包商，协助他们加强质量体系及管理，进而达到国际水准，从而也培养了一批中国的优质产品制造商及施工队伍等。同时，在Fluor工作期间，我也结识了一批国际业主中国代表方的朋友。

2016年夏天，我有幸加入CNOOD，当时是负责海外工程项目的采购出口，涉

home and abroad for the next 22 years. I was dispatched to Saudi Arabia for 2 years and to the United States for 1 year to handle the procurement and outsourcing of CTCI's engineering projects in China. Required by work, I had been traveling in the Middle East, Asia, Europe and North America, thus meeting and dealing with a lot of international professionals and knowing better how to complete EPC projects.

After joining Fluor China in early 2002, I was responsible for procurement management, contract management and development and management of Chinese suppliers. During this period, I was also involved in mining, paper-making, pharmaceuticals, offshore oil drilling engineering and module manufacturing operations in addition to petrochemical engineering, power plants and public works construction. To meet Fluor's global engineering needs and reduce construction costs, I developed various Chinese suppliers and contractors according to Fluor's policy requirements, and assisted them to strengthen their quality system and management for compliance with international standards. Hence, a batch of Chinese high-quality product manufacturers and construction teams have been developed. My work experience in Fluor also allowed me to meet the Chinese representatives of international clients.

In the summer of 2016, I was honored to join CNOOD, a company specialized

及各类产品和设备。在这5年多的时间里，公司已经成功转型成为中小型总承包公司。在这个成立近12年，员工平均年龄在30多岁的年轻公司，我见证了公司的转变以及多元化经营。我看到在CNOOD董事长Dennis的个人领导魅力、大爱、无私、身先士卒品质的带领下，公司全员的努力下，CNOOD得以逐步完成转型。我也见证了一些几乎难以完成的项目顺利结束，尤其是在2020年新冠肺炎疫情暴发的状况下，完成了海外的水处理总包项目、码头建设工程专业分包项目、高难度高质量大型钢结构专业分包项目、海洋养殖业海洋船舶类项目的设计建造、海上风电项目以及完成了大型项目的报价投标工作等。我也见识到公司年轻有为的CEO Fay，相关项目经理，如Billy、Chris、Lloyd、Peter等，见证他们个人能力的发挥，他们工作的认真，让我佩服。

早自1998年，我个人来中国大陆工作已有20多年，我亲自见证了祖国的进步、繁荣、富强，各项建设突飞猛进，制

in procurement and export of products and equipment for overseas engineering projects. Over the past 5 years, CNOOD has successfully transformed into a small and medium-sized EPC company. While working for this young company with a history of 12 years and an average employee age of 30, I have witnessed its transformation and diversification. I have seen how CNOOD, under the leadership of the charismatic, caring and selfless Chairman Dennis and the concerted efforts of all employees, gradually completes its transformation. I have also seen how some of the seemingly impossible projects are completed, designed and approached, especially during the outbreak of COVID-19, including the completion of overseas water treatment EPC project, the terminal construction specialized subcontract project and the high difficulty and high quality large steel structure specialized subcontract project, the design and construction of the marine aquaculture industry and marine ship projects, and the quotation and bidding of the offshore wind power project and other large projects. Furthermore, I have been a witness to and an admirer of how the young and promising CEO Fay Lee leads the project managers Billy Gu, Chris Lee, Lloyd Zhang and Peter Tao, and how they give play to their capabilities and work conscientiously.

After working in Chinese mainland for about 20 years since 1998, I have witnessed the progress and prosperity of

造商、承包商能力的快速提升（特别是质量与安全管理）。身为中国人，我深感骄傲，对 CNOOD 的成功也是如此。我非常愿意持续将个人的经验奉献给 CNOOD，也深信不久的将来，在创造开心、相互关心、共创共治共享的经营理念下，CNOOD 会在全球大放异彩。

最后要特别感谢 CNOOD 全体同事给予我这位将近 70 岁的老人的关怀和呵护，让我在这 5 年的工作中十分愉快，尤其感谢 Billy 对我工作的支持、推展和协助。

the motherland, the astounding advances of constructions and the rapid capability improvement of manufacturers and contractors (especially in quality and safety management). I am proud to be Chinese and to be part of the successful development of CNOOD. Hence, it's my pleasure to continuously contribute my experience to CNOOD. I am convinced that CNOOD will shine in the world in the near future under the business concept of happiness, mutual care, joint creation, joint governance and sharing.

Lastly, I would like to extend my special thanks to all employees of CNOOD for their care, especially to Billy Gu for his support, promotion and assistance to my work. It has been a delightful five-year journey in CNOOD for me, a senior approaching 70.

陈祖平
Paul Chen

1952 年 10 月 6 日生于中国台湾省，祖籍山东。从事工程设计、采购、建造相关工作 43 年。2016 年 8 月加入 CNOOD。

Born in Taiwan, China on June 6, 1959. Ancestral home: Shandong Province. 43 years of engineering experience, including design, procurement and construction. He joined CNOOD in August 2016.

后疫情时代业务发展计划
——非常必要还是浪费时间？

Business Plan for Post-Pandemic
—Is It Necessary or Waste of Time?

■ Amir Tafti

自新冠肺炎疫情发生以来，疫情一直是影响全球发展的主要因素之一，导致全球GDP增长速度降至2008年金融危机以来的最低水平。据国际货币基金组织（IMF）研究显示，此次疫情与2008年金融危机存在着一个根本区别：2008年金融危机波及的大多数是发达国家，而此次受全球性疫情影响最严重的则是发展中国家。

尽管全球注入25万亿美元的流动性用于公共疫苗研发、接种的时间要早于预期，但要去除并改善疫情造成的损失还需要很长时间。疫情已导致广泛性失业，并给贫困国家甚至发展中国家带来了巨额债务。

In the past few months and even now, COVID-19 is acting as one of the main rulers of the world, and GDP in the world fell to its lowest level since the financial crisis in 2008. But this one is more tragic for world's economy, because according to IMF research, one fundamental difference exists between the current pandemic and the 2008 economic crisis: while the recession in 2008 involved mostly rich countries, this time it is the poor and developing countries that are most affected by this global crisis.

Although right now the injection of $25 trillion in liquidity into the global economy for public vaccinations happens earlier than expected, it will take a long time to heal and improve the wounds of this disease, which has led to widespread unemployment and imposed huge debts

国际货币基金组织研究中心预测，2021年全球至少有2亿人将会面临失业，其中大多数失业人员来自发展中国家。据预测，在这些国家中10%的中产阶级公民将加入低收入和贫穷行列。

随着这些国家的发展形势，大多数的公司，特别是民营公司，会跌至第二或第三档的情况，甚至有些公司会面临破产的悲惨境地。

1. 背景介绍

尽管在疫情期间，许多组织都迅速作出调整，以史上最敏捷的速度采取行动，但即使到如今，疫情带来的危机以及疫情后的态势仍未明晰，企业决策者们也在担心企业是否可以恢复如初。

on poor, even developing countries.

IMF Research Center forecasts showed that at least 200 million people around the world will be dragged down the economic ladder in 2021, mostly in the poor and developing countries. It is predicted that 10 percent of the middle-class citizens of these communities will become low-income and poor.

Following the countries, most of the companies, especially private companies will fall to the second or third tiers, and some of them will even face tragic conditions such as bankruptcy.

1. Introduction

Although during the pandemic, many organizations rapidly adapted, moving with more agility than ever before, now, as we hang in the limbo between the crisis and a post-pandemic reality, CEOs are concerned about whether their organizations will snap back into old ways of working.

现在，各大企业的决策者越来越关注疫情对企业本身以及企业战略和活动的影响，特别是对员工的影响。数据显示，各组织面临着非常严重的人力资源危机，决策者们不应低估后疫情时代会面临的困难。员工焦虑、社会环境、组织文化等障碍会延长企业走出困境的时间。

在后疫情时代，企业决策者面临的主要问题是如何在成本与市场压力和季度盈利目标之间取得平衡。此外，另一个根本挑战是劳动力的技能差距。

每家公司都将步入后疫情新时代，但需要通过制定全新的合理的商业计划规划发展速度与规模。

2. 后疫情时代的商业计划

（1）业务发展计划的一般定义。

商业计划是一份正式的书面文件，包含企业目标、目标实现方法以及目标实现时间表。它还描述了业务的性质、组织的背景信息、组织的财务预测以及实现既定目标的战略。从整体上看，业务发展计划就像一个为业务发展提供方向的路线图。

Right now, CEOs are increasingly concerned about the impact of the pandemic on their companies, strategies and activities, especially on the employees. Figures show that the human resources crisis in organizations is serious and CEOs should not underestimate the difficulties in the post-pandemic era ahead. Employee anxiety, social conditions, organizational culture and other obstacles can prolong this path for companies.

The main issue is how CEOs can balance the cost with market pressures and quarterly earnings targets in the post-pandemic era. In addition, another fundamental challenge is the skill gap in the workforce.

Every company can move into a new era (post-pandemic), but need to define the basis of speed and scale by preparing the new logical business plan.

2. Business plan for post-pandemic

(1) Common definition of business plan.

A business plan is a formal written document containing the goals of a business, the methods for attaining those goals, and the time-frame for the achievement of the goals. It also describes the nature of the business, background information on the organization, the organization's financial projections, and the strategies it intends to implement to achieve the stated targets. In its entirety, this document serves as a road-map (a plan) that provides direction to the

（2）制定后疫情时代商业计划是否会浪费时间？

或许有些公司会质疑是否真的有必要制定一份商业计划来提升和发展后疫情时代的业务。让人感到奇怪的是研究表明这个问题的答案既是肯定的，又是否定的。

根据对一些受访企业的表现进行研究，那些预测发展未来并试图"防范于未然"的企业在遇到问题时，被迫采取非既定策略的另一种策略。在后疫情时代，这种形势将更加复杂。因此，最好的策略是静观其变，并为每个临时出现的问题找到一个具体的解决方案。显然，我们不应该浪费时间去预测商业环境和市场形势，而是应该更早地进入市场，通过市场分析"应该做什么和如何做"。

(2) Is it a waste of time to prepare a business plan for post-pandemic era?

Perhaps companies also wonder if they need to have a well-planned business plan to improve and develop the business during the post-pandemic era. It may be strange to know that research conducted to answer this question confirms both "YES" and "NO."

Citing to performance of some of the businesses surveyed, research has concluded that businesses that predict the future and try to "cure the event before they happen" are forced to adopt a strategy other than what they have already determined when they encounter the issues. This situation will be more complicated for the post-pandemic era. Therefore, it is better to wait and find a specific solution for each issue improvised. It is clear that instead of wasting time on predicting business climate and market conditions, we should enter the market sooner so that the market itself tells us "what & how to do".

相反，一些研究表明，预先编制疫情后的商业计划不仅不会浪费时间，还会由于多方面原因增加成功和业务发展的可能性。

（3）制定业务发展计划是否可助力企业成功？

根据其他研究和数据，银行和金融机构为制定有效合理的商业计划的企业提供金融信贷的概率翻了一番。此外，大约有70%的制定了商业计划的公司的业务已经在增加，而没有制定商业计划的公司，只有40%的公司的业务在增加。

（4）商业计划可以带来哪些变化？

现在需要提出的问题是，制定商业计划如何增加成功的机会？为了回答这个问题，我们需要明确制定后疫情时代具体商业计划的主要原则。

① 衡量创意的可执行性。

一份有效合理的商业计划展示了实施不同创意的能力。通过对这些创意进行统计分析及可行性分析，确定其可操作性，从一开始就放弃那些不能具体执行的创业细节。

On the contrary, some research showed us that having pre-prepared business plans for the post-pandemic era not only won't be a waste of time, but will also increase the likelihood of success and business development for a number of reasons.

(3) Is having a business plan effective in corporate success?

According to some different research and data obtained, the probability of banks and financial institutions providing financial credit doubles for businesses that have effective logical business plans. Also, around 70 percent of businesses with business plans have been able to expand their activities, while for companies that do not have codified business plans, it is only 40 percent.

(4) What changes does a business plan make?

Now the question that needs to be asked is: how does having a business plan increase the chances of success? To answer this question, try to mention the main reasons to prepare the specific business plan for the post-pandemic era:

① Measuring the level of excecutability of ideas.

One effective and logical business plan demonstrates the ability to implement different ideas. By statistically examining and operationalizing the ideas, their operability is determined and ideas that cannot be converted into specific executive details will be removed from the very beginning.

② 明确管理层决策框架。

对于未制定合理的商业计划的公司，面对后疫情时代的新形势，决策者可能会感到困惑，因为没有固定的标准可以衡量他们的决策，各管理人员将根据自己的远见和想象来看待问题。但是如果有一个具体的商业计划，一切行动都必须根据总体框架来确定以获得批准。

事实上，商业计划将作为决策的基准，公司在面对新形势时总会采取朝着已知方向的战略。在这种情况下，您将根据业务活动的真正潜力，而非根据业务活动的整体印象或业务目标来决策。

② Clarifying the framework of manager's decisions.

In companies that do not have logical business plans, facing new situations such as the post-pandemic era can confuse decision makers because there are no fixed criteria to weight their decisions with, and each manager looks at the issue according to their vision and imagination. But if there is a specific business plan, everything has to adapt to its overall framework for approval.

In fact, a business plan will act as the benchmark stone of decisions, and the company's strategy in the face of new situations will always move in a direction that is already known. In this case, you will make decisions that are based on the true potential of your activity, not the overall impression or aspirations as a dream in your businesses.

③ 获得投资者和金融机构的信任。

如今基于疫情形势及后疫情时代形势，所有投资者及金融机构都采取了保守的发展策略。制定详细而现实的商业计划，需囊括及分析成本、收入、合同等企业金融信息，将有助于您获得投资者和金融机构的信任。当然，正如详细的商业计划可助力企业发展，不明确、笼统，特别是乐观的商业计划可能会适得其反，无法为投资者带来一定的确定性。

④ 为管理层及员工规划清晰的发展前景。

包括公司管理层、员工在内的所有人员都清楚大家要实现的共同目标时，就会提高成员的绩效，提升工作满意度。如果制定商业计划，并向企业成员解释其特点和目标，那么就有可能将具有不同利益的个人团结起来，努力实现这些目标。

（5）结论。

制定后疫情时代商业计划似乎不仅不浪费时间，而且非常必要。但是如果商业计划基于不切实际的幻想或不合理的目标制定，那么将会毁掉企业。

③ Gaining the trust of investors and financial institutions.

Right now, based on the pandemic situation and surely during the post-pandemic era, all investors and financial institutions move ahead conservatively. Having a detailed and realistic business plan that contains and analyzes the financial details of your business well such as costs, revenues, contracts, etc. helps you gain their trust. Of course, as much as having a detailed business plan benefits your business, having an uncertain, general and especially optimistic business plan can bring the opposite result and cannot provide such a level of certainty for the investors.

④ Creating clear outlook for all managers and employees.

In fact, when managers, employees and all personnel of a company have a clear idea of what common goals they are working to achieve, it in itself improves the performance of members and increases their job satisfaction. By having a business plan and explaining its characteristics and objectives to the members of the complex, it is possible to unite individuals with different interests in an effort to achieve the goals.

(5) Conclusion

As a conclusion, it seems that preparation of a business plan for the post-pandemic era not only isn't a waste of time but also is necessary. But if this business plan is prepared based on inaccessible dreams or illogical goals, along with other factors,

因此，我们应该牢记的是：由专业人员根据实际情况制定疫情期间及后疫情时代商业计划可轻松实现守业。

can cause the failure of a business.

We should remember that it is easy to safely defend our company during the pandemic and post-pandemic era by preparing and formulating a business plan by skilled people based on the real situations.

Amir Tafti

飞行器工程本科毕业后，我在不同行业领域的政府部门和私营企业工作过，拥有超过 30 年的专业经验，尤其是在工业领域。回首往昔，有好几个理由让我相信自己是一个幸运的人。主要的一个理由是：我在同一个政府机构工作了 20 年，负责对我们国家不同的项目进行审计。我的第一份工作就是在政府部门，工作期间，我从一名普通的职员升为最高级别的经理。我学到了很多东西，并得以积累大量相关经验。此后，私营行业领域同样也为我提供了一个良好的、充满挑战的平台，使我能够成长为合格人才。现在我已经 57 岁了，很荣幸成为施璐德团队的一员。我将尽我所能，把我的经验和知识传授给同事们，帮助营造一个更好的竞争环境。

I am Amir Tafti, with a Bachelor of Science degree in aircraft engineering and more than 30 years of special work experience in different sectors (especially in industrial fields) in both the government and the private sector. When I look back on my past, I find myself to be a lucky person in many ways. First of all, I worked for 20 years in one special governmental office, responsible for auditing the different projects in my country. It was my first and last governmental job. I started as a common employee and ended up as a top-level manger, I learned a lot and collected a huge amount of related experience. After that, even the private sector I worked in provided a good and challengeable platform for me to grow to be qualified person. Now 57 years old, it is my pleasure to join the CNOOD team and do my best to transfer my experience and knowledge to my colleagues to create a better competitive environment.

静女其姝

My Beloved Daughter

■ Andy Wei

夏季满园清香的栀子花告知了你的到来；秋季色彩斑斓的枫叶送给你祝福；冬季凌寒独放的蜡梅见证了你的发育；春季暖色三月的早樱迎来了你的降生。期盼着带你去看落叶缤纷，陪你去听莺声燕语，逛菊花展、赏郁金香。顾村的樱花也在期盼着你。

十个月的呵护和期盼等来了初见你时的心动，初为人父的我在见到你的那一刻深切地感受到了血脉相连的触动，这就是我需要用一生来呵护的人。你用响亮的哭声宣示你的到来，妈妈用肌肤的温度抚平了你初来乍到的紧张，爸爸将所有人的祝福转达给你。我们感受到了，这就是幸福。

The fragrant gardenias in summer announced your arrival; the maple leaves in autumn blessed you; the blossoming wintersweet in winter bore witness to your growth in Mommy's womb; the spring cherry in March welcomed your birth. With you Daddy watched the falling leaves, listened to the tweets of birds, went to the chrysanthemum show and appreciated the tulips. The cherry blossoms in Gucun were expecting to see you.

After ten months of care and anticipation, you were finally born, which stirred my soul. The moment Daddy laid eyes on you, Daddy felt the continuity of the blood line. You are the one Daddy will spend the rest of my life protecting. You announced your arrival with loud cries. Mommy soothed your nerves with the temperature on her skin. Daddy sent the best regards from others to you. Mommy and Daddy felt what happiness is.

在你初次睁眼懵懂好奇地打量这个世界时，爸爸也在目不转睛地看着你，从你纯净的眼里看到了光，相信你也从爸爸的眼里感受到了爱，从此以后你就是爸妈的恒星。你无意识的一个笑容可以令全家人高兴、你每一个难受的表情也令全家人揪心，手忙脚乱中懂得了与你沟通，我们是围绕着你的行星。

爸爸替你读了《三字经》和《弟子规》，妈妈为你描绘了诗和远方。我们已做好呵护你、陪伴你的准备，我们还将学习如何去爱你、教育你，使你拥有一个快乐的童年、健康的体魄以及自信的笑、自律的心、自强的品质。

我们一起学习、一起成长，往后余生，请多指教。

When you opened your eyes and watched the world with curiosity, Daddy looked at you eagerly and intently. Daddy saw the light in your pure eyes and believed that you too saw the love in Daddy's eyes. From now on you will be the fixed star of Mommy and Daddy as we will be the planets revolving around you. An unconscious smile of you would make the whole family happy, and a painful expression of you would sadden the whole family. As we tried to take good care of you, we learned how to communicate with you.

Daddy has read the *Three-Character Primer* and *Disciple Gauge* for you, and Mommy has painted you a poetic future. We have learned how to take care of and accompany you, and we will learn how to love and cducate you and give you a happy childhood, a healthy body and the qualities of confidence, self-discipline and self-improvement.

We will learn and grow together. Please guide Daddy for the rest of our lives together.

魏 坤 Andy Wei	一位正值而立之年且初为人父的青年。 A young man in his thirties and also a new father.

新冠肺炎疫情给我们带来的教训
Lessons from the COVID-19 Pandemic

■ Patricia Yaber Tacchini

从 2020 年到 2021 年年初，有太多的人面临着疫情防控措施带来的不便，不能互相探望，不能上班，不能上学，不能在公共场所见面。在危险时刻，我们本能地想要靠近家人和朋友，握住他们的手，拥抱他们，但现在我们只能忍住，因为每一个身体接触的行为，每一个慈爱和同情的肢体表达，都可能带来疾病和死亡。

我们多久忽视我们存在的不确定性？我们多久忽略了自己的脆弱性，假装掌握着自己的命运？新冠肺炎疫情向我们表明，我们错得多么离谱。事实上，我们面对的是人类存在的极度不确定性和人类生命的极度脆弱性。我们当中的很多人竟然时常认为自己是世界的最高主宰。

During last year and up to beginning of this year, too many people have endured the inconveniences of lockdowns, unable to visit one another, unable to go to work, unable to attend school, and unable to meet one another in public places. At times of existential danger, we instinctively desire to be close to our family and friends, to hold their hands and embrace them, but now we have been forbidden to do so, for every act of physical contact — every expression of physical loving-kindness and compassion — could bring illness and death.

How often have we ignored the uncertainty of our existence? How often have we ignored our vulnerability, by pretending that we are in control of our destinies? The COVID-19 pandemic shows us how wrong we were. The truth is that we have been confronted with the true uncertainty of human existence and the true vulnerability of human life. How

直面生命中最基本的问题：我们是为了什么而存在？我们这辈子都干了些什么？如果有机会，我们还希望做些什么？谁对我们的生活真的重要？我们真正珍惜的是什么？这场疫情让我们看到了一些痛苦的现实：如果我们知道谁对我们真的重要，我们真正珍惜什么，为什么我们花那么少的时间去追求这些东西？

新冠肺炎疫情让我们看到：浪费生命，无休止地争夺财富、地位和权力是多么可怕；没有认识到身边人的价值是多么可怕——不仅仅是家人和朋友，不仅仅是同事和同胞，还有面前的陌生人。如果任何时候都不尊重生命的神圣，给予所有生灵应有的尊重、感性和关怀，以赋予我们生命的意义，将是多么地可怕。

新冠肺炎疫情让我们看到自由的价值，属于自己及身边人的自由，包括行动的自由、与所爱之人在一起的自由、有尊严和安全地生活的自由。最重要的是，新冠肺炎疫情让我们认识到我们建立的所有共同组织的真正目的的重要性，这些组织的宗旨是为人类的需要和目的服务——不仅仅是为个人服务，而且是为社会服务。

often have so many of us believed that we are supreme masters of the world around us?

We are brought face to face with the most basic questions of life: What are we here for? What have we done with our lives? What do we yet wish to do if given the opportunity? Who is truly important to our lives? What is it that we truly cherish? The pandemic leads us to some painful insights: If we know who is truly important to us and what we truly cherish, then why have we spent so little of our lives pursuing them?

The coronavirus shows us how terrible it really is to waste our lives, embroiled in endless battles for wealth and status and power. How terrible it really is not to recognize the value in the people around us, not just our family and friends, not just colleagues and fellow citizens, but also strangers in front of us. It is terrible not giving our lives meaning — every hour of every day — by honoring the sacredness of life and according all living things with the respect, sensitivity and care that they deserve.

The COVID-19 pandemic demonstrates to us the value of freedom — the freedom to move, to be with those we love, to live in dignity and security — for ourselves and for those around us. Above all, it shows us the importance of recognizing the true purpose of all our common organizations, called to serve human needs and purposes, not just as individuals, also as the society.

在我们的大多数努力中，我们都是相互依赖的。一个人的成功离不开与他人的合作。我们在地方、区域和国家等不同层面上开展合作。新冠肺炎疫情凸显了忽视相互依存和全球合作重要性的危险。它向我们清晰地表明，所有人类都在同一条船上。因此，我们需要彼此生存。

多年以来形成的美德让我们辛勤工作、诚实相待和信任彼此，这是我们能够在和平中共同成长的方式。人类是一种主要适合合作的社会动物，这一点从来未曾改变。这是一个永远不会消失的根本性挑战。我们所能做的就是认识到这一点，保持警惕，调整我们自己以适应所面临的巨大挑战。

新冠肺炎疫情将我们置于危险之中，迫使我们认识到我们最基本的需求和我们的最高价值。它迫使我们去欣赏那些社会作用往往被低估的人的真正价值：护士、医院护理员、超市收银员、送货员、许多向老人和弱势群体提供帮助的无名陌生人。

新冠肺炎疫情展现了世界各地社会无处不在的善意和仁慈。它让医院和护理院出现了无数无私的英雄行为。它促使我们

In most of our endeavors, we are interdependent. One individual cannot succeed without the cooperation of others. We cooperate at many different scales — local, regional and national. The COVID-19 pandemic highlights the danger of ignoring our interdependence and the importance of global cooperation. It shows us with crystal clarity that all of humanity is in the same boat; therefore, we need each other to survive.

The virtues that have formed over the many years promote hard work, honesty and trust so that we can growth together in peace. It has always been the case that humans are social creatures, who are suited primarily for cooperation. This is a fundamental challenge that will never go away. All we can do is to be aware of it, remain vigilant, adjust our narratives to the magnitude of the challenges we face, and continually adapt ourselves.

The COVID-19 pandemic lays our lives bare and forces us to appreciate our most essential needs and our highest values. It forces us to appreciate the true value of many people whose roles in the society tend to be undervalued: the nurses, the hospital orderlies, the people sitting at the checkout counters in supermarkets, and the delivery personnel, and the many nameless strangers who suddenly offer help to the old and vulnerable.

The pandemic has revealed a vast sea of kindness and benevolence in our communities around the world. It has led

中的许多人利用我们最强大的力量去为我们最伟大的目标服务,突然为我们的生活赋予全新的、鼓舞人心的意义。

to countless acts of selfless heroism in hospitals and care homes. It has impelled many of us to use our greatest strengths to serve our greatest purposes, suddenly giving our lives new and inspiring meaning.

星光不问赶路人，时光不负有心人

The Stars Don't Ask the Travelers and Time Never Lets the Determined Down

■ Loreen Luo

很多时候我们没办法走到自己能量的边界，是因为我们很早就给自己下定论"我做不到"。或者是根据周围的声音和经验，告诉我们"你做不到"。

自2011年，我来上海读研，然后毕业后工作，至今已有十年整，有过成就感，也有过自我实现，但随着时间的推移，感觉自己还是遇到了瓶颈，甚至偶尔也会觉得自己"一事无成"，达不到自己的要求。特别是在离开CNOOD的那两年时间，自己变得胆小和没有自信，也许在外人看来并非真的如此，但是总逃不过自己内心，少了那种"初生牛犊不怕虎"的胆识与决断力，开始变得畏首畏尾。感觉自己需要学习了，一种沉下心来的系统学习，通过学习来给自己这些年实践中遇到的问题解答，通过学习梳理巩固实践中积累的好的经验。于是在2020年11月份，

Most of the time we can't push ourselves to the limit of our energy. That's because we have long decided that "I can't do it" or surrounding people and previous experience tell us that "You can't do it."

It has been ten years since I came to Shanghai to start my postgraduate study in 2011. I had felt a sense of accomplishment and self-realization. As time went by, however, I still felt I had hit a wall or occasionally considered myself "accomplishing nothing" and failing to live up to my own expectations. During the two years after my departure from CNOOD in particular, I became timid and non-confident. Perhaps that's not the case in the eyes of others, but I couldn't turn a blind eye to my inner self. Without the audacity like newborn calves not

我做了一个很仓促又很胆大的决定，报考 2020 年 12 月 26 日的全国工商管理专业研究生（MBA）的统考。

一旦树立了这个目标，一切就变得紧张起来，距离考试仅仅只有 20 天的准备时间（很早就敲定了 12 月 5 日的婚期，办完婚礼才正式准备复习）。我要如何在不影响正常上班的前提下，来完成这个看起来似乎不可能的任务呢？如何完成"20 天复习考上研究生"这个项目？

1. 明确目标

给自己设置一个切实通过努力可以实现的目标，只有一个月时间就不要想着考 200 多分了（总分 300），目标在国家 A 区线 175 分以上就好。

2. 分解目标执行步骤，构思复习计划

首先客观分析自己所处的位置，MBA 全国统考一共考 2 门，英语（总分 100）和管理综合（总分 200，涵盖数学 75 分，逻辑题 60 分，两篇论说文写作 65 分）。由于时间真的太紧张了，除去工作和睡觉，每天只有 10 小时左右集中复

afraid of tigers and the decisiveness, I became overcautious. I felt that I needed to pursue further study, settle down and learn systematically. Through learning, I hoped to answer the questions in practice over the years and consolidate the good practices. Therefore, I made a rush yet bold decision last November by signing up for the national MBA entrance examination scheduled on December 26, 2020.

After the goal was set, everything became tense. There were about 20 days left for the examination (as my wedding day was long set on December 5, I could only prepared for the examination after the wedding). How could I accomplish this seemingly impossible task without affecting my daily work? How could I finish the project of "preparing for the MBA entrance examination in 20 days"?

1. Setting a well-defined goal

I first set a practical goal which could be realized by hard work. Instead of planning to achieve a score of 200 points (full mark 300 points) in the examination to be taken one month later, I aimed for a score of 175 points, the national A score line.

2. Working out the goal execution steps and preparation plan

First, I objectively analyzed my situation. The national MBA entrance examination consists of two subjects: English (full mark 100 points) and General Management (full mark 200 points, composed of 75 points for mathematics, 60 points for logic questions and 65 points for two essays). Time was really pressing as I only had 10 hours to prepare for the examination every day after working and sleeping. Therefore, a preparation plan which highlights the key points and priorities must be worked out. Then I rapidly analyzed my "strong points." Over the years I have been using English as my working language, so I decided not to review English except for memorizing the words. Shanbay was used to quickly memorize 1000 words for the examination every day to get an impression. In addition to English, essay writing was also my strong point as I had a good writing foundation. Though never engaged in specialized essay writing, I was confident in it and decided to start the review and mock test two days before the examination date. Logic questions were a "medium" challenge for me as I had not learned about them before. However, this part requires no foundation, and a breakthrough within a short period of time could help me get half of the points. Therefore, I needed to obtain a steady score for this part and spent at least 60% of my time ou reviewing logic questions. Mathematics was my "weakest link." In mathematics, I could only get how much I put in and had no gift. Hence, I could only work hard on this subject. In consideration of the tight schedule and wide range, I adopted the half giving up strategy in mathematics. After quickly going through the textbook,

习，必须重点突出，主次分明地制定复习计划。迅速分析出自己基础好的"长板"，这些年一直将英语作为工作语言，英语决定直接不复习了，只记单词，每天快速用扇贝记单词刷考研单词1 000个，用最快的速度，只求有印象。除了英语，中文两篇论说文写作也算自己的强项，因为自己写作基础比较好，虽然之前没接触过，但是有信心，只在考前两天开始准备和模拟。逻辑题是我的"中板"，因为之前从来没专门学过，但是这门课不需要基础，只要短时间集中突破，就可以拿到一半的分数。故集中火力，把逻辑这个分数稳住，花了至少60%的时间来复习逻辑。数学就是我的最大"短板"了，在数学方面我是那种付出多少才能收获多少的人，没有特别的天赋，只能靠努力。但是这次时间特别紧张，数学考试范围又很广，我采取半放弃策略，快速翻阅一遍教材，了解一些基本公式，直接上手做真题，力求把真题的知识点搞懂，鉴于时间紧张，只准备做4套真题。就这样取长保短，力求过线。

I memorized some basic formulas and began doing mock exercises, striving to fully understand the knowledge points in these exercises. Pressed for time, I planned to do 4 examination papers. In this way I intended to give full play to my strong points and deliver acceptable performance in my weak points, so as to achieve the preset goal.

3. 坚决执行计划，一步一个脚印

考研的日期既定，自己的目标和客观情况也已既定，只能勇往直前了。办完婚礼，送走宾客，马上就收拾好行李，直接住到公司隔壁的酒店了，我要抓住一切可以挤出来的时间，每一天每一分每一秒我都要严格按照计划执行，完成这个艰巨的任务。作息时间：早上5:30起床，学习到9:20，用最快速度洗漱吃早饭到公司9:30；中午吃饭时间，马上回酒店学习2小时，边学习边吃外卖；晚上下班，马上回酒店，点好外卖，学习到晚上11:45左右。

3. Resolutely executing the plan step by step

Now that the examination date, my goal and objective conditions had been set, I could only go ahead. The moment I saw off the guests after the wedding ceremony, I packed and moved to the hotel next to CNOOD. I had to seize the time I squeezed out and rigorously execute my plan down to every second to accomplish this arduous task. I generally got up at 5:30 a.m. and studied until 9:20 a.m. Then I washed up, had breakfast and arrived at the Company at 9:30 a.m. During the 2-hour lunch break, I returned to the hotel and studied while having a takeout. As soon as I clocked out in the afternoon, I headed back to the hotel, ordered a takeout and studied until 11:45 p.m.

4. 不到最后一刻，不想任何消极的事情

虽然备考仅仅只有20天，但是真的每天都想放弃。高强度的复习节奏，新旧知识点轮番袭来。逻辑虽然不难，但是真的需要特别花时间和精力去理解的，比较费脑。复习数学时，更感觉自己失忆了，

4. Thinking nothing negative until the last moment

Although there were only 20 days to prepare for the examination, I did want to give up every day. At such an intensive reviewing pace, I went through the new and old knowledge points in turns. The

明明曾经那么熟悉的公式和题目，现在完全陌生。做真题更是痛苦，MBA考试特点就是没有特别难题，但是题量特别大，要求速度非常快。可是，真的没有时间让我痛苦和胡思乱想，既然已经选择了，已经开始了，就不要想结果，坚持去考试，就是一种成功。脑海里回荡Dennis以前在常熟工厂项目上对我说的话："不要想任何消极的事情，只有一个念头，就是往前走。"不管了，死马当活马医吧，一定不能当逃兵。

5. 全力以赴

考试的那个周六（圣诞节）很冷，定好了早上4点的闹钟，5点出发，因为防疫要求，需要提前很早去考场。5点50分，抵达考场，心情很平静，因为在既定的时间，自己已经尽力了，为自己高兴，没有放弃，坚持到了考场。考研就是这样的一场与自己的战斗，一路上都有人放弃，即使到了考场，上午考完，下午的考试你的邻桌可能就不来了，所以战胜的不是别人，而是自己。

logic questions were not difficult, but it did need time and energy to understand. It was brain-racking. When I reviewed mathematics, I had the illusion of memory loss. The formulas and questions with which I was so familiar were now strangers to me. It was excruciating to do the mock questions. The MBA entrance examination is known for the enormous amount of questions despite having no particular difficult questions, which requires a fast answering speed. However, there was no time for me to feel the pain and entertain all sorts of ideas. Now that I had chosen to sign up for the examination and started the preparation, I didn't have to think about the result. As long as I held out until the examination, it was success in a sense. I often thought of what Dennis said to me in the Changshu Plant Project, "Don't think of anything negative. Just have one thought. Go ahead." Make every possible effort and never be a quitter.

5. Going all out

It was a cold Saturday on the examination date during the Christmas holiday. I set the clock at 4:00 a.m. and set out at 5:00 a.m. as we were required to arrive at the examination venue early due to epidemic prevention and control. I arrived at the examination venue at 5:50 a.m. and felt calm. That's because I had tried my best within the given time limit, and I felt happy for myself for not giving up and holding out until the examination. The MBA entrance examination was

"星光不问赶路人，时光不负有心人"，最终我侥幸飘过了国家线，每部分分数的呈现和我当时取长保短的计划预期几乎一致，完成了自己设置的目标，进入上海外国语大学的复试环节。由于我的笔试分数刚过线，所以是否能被录取，复试（面试）就是最关键的环节，我必须逆袭，复试分数要很高，才能挤进为数不多的录取名额。

复试主要由 5 分钟的英语交流，加上 20 分钟与 7 位面试老师的聊天式问答组成。老师问："你未来对自己的规划和目标是什么，上外 MBA 可以给你带来什么？"我自信地答道："我未来的目标就是做一名跨国公司的 CEO，上外 MBA 培养学生的目标就是'无国界管理者'，这正是这些年来我一直在做和未来一直想做的事情。"之所以自信从容，因为这就是 CNOOD 和老池一直在践行和倡导的，这些年一直在耳濡目染的。老师继续提问："举例你在工作中被很多人认为很难，但你做到的事情？"我马上答："把一批油套管运送到伊拉克北部库尔德，由于伊拉克

a battle against yourself. There were people giving up halfway, even in the examination room. The examinee next to you might not sit for the examination in the afternoon after the examination in the morning. Therefore, you needed to beat yourself, instead of others.

"The stars don't ask the travelers and time never lets the determined down." Eventually I scored slightly higher than the national A score line. The score for each part was almost the same as I expected. I accomplished my pre-set goal and entered into the enrollment interview of Shanghai International Studies University. As my score in the written examination just surpassed the score line, the enrollment interview was crucial to whether I could be enrolled into the MBA program. Therefore, I had to achieve an extremely high score in the interview to be one of the handful interviewees to be accepted.

The interview was composed of a 5-min English communication and a 20-min Q&A chat with 7 interviewers. One of the interviewers asked, "What's your plan and goal for your future? What can the MBA of Shanghai International Studies University bring you?" I replied with confidence, "My future goal is becoming the CEO of a transnational corporation. The MBA of Shanghai International Studies University is intended to train 'managers without borders.' This is exactly what I have been doing and will be doing in the future." The reason

长年战乱,我们必须把货物先用集装箱运到土耳其,卸下来再用卡车通过土耳其与伊拉克北部口岸城市,一路经过战乱区,且需要协调好两次清关和在伊拉克迅速卸车问题,因为土耳其卡车必须尽快返回土耳其,不然将产生大量压车费用。"老师问:"从你的简历看到,你从 CNOOD 这家公司出去了,后来又回来了,可以跟我们分享一下原因吗?"我回答:"如果把时间线拉长,假设我站在自己 40 岁的节点来回头看,可能最大的遗憾和后悔就是离开了期望和帮助自己成长的良师益友,离开了一个希望让自己持续成长的环境……"

约半小时的面试结束,我可以感觉到面试组的老师们对我的回答和经历还挺满意的。直到前几天上外官宣拟录取公示,看到了复试成绩,才发现我竟然是复试(含预面试)全国第一,286.65 分,总分应该是 300 分。这无疑是对我个人,对我在 CNOOD 这些年的经历和形成理念、价值观的最大肯定。因为参与 MBA 复试和

that I gave such an assertive answer is that this is what CNOOD and Mr. CHI have been advocating and I have been under such influence. The interviewer continued, "Can you give an example of things which are considered difficult by many people but you have accomplished at work?" I gave an immediate answer, "I shipped a batch of oil casing and tubing pipes to Kurd, Northern Iraq. As Iraq is a war-torn country, we had to ship the goods in containers to Turkey first and then transferr them to trucks and go through the war zone to the port city in Northern Iraq. Twice customs clearance must be properly coordinated, and the goods must be quickly unloaded in Iraq as the Turkish trucks must head back to Turkey as soon as possible to avoid a large amount of truck overdue costs." Another interviewer asked, "As can be seen from your resume, you left CNOOD and then joined it again. Can you tell us about the reason for it?" I answered, "If the timeline was stretched longer to my age of 40, my biggest regret might possibly be leaving the mentors who expect and help me grow and an environment which hopes for my continuous growth …"

After the interview, I could feel that the interviewers were quite satisfied with my answers and experience. It was not until a few days earlier when the official website of Shanghai International Studies University released the proposed enrollment list that I saw my interview result. I was surprised to find that I

预复试的同学全国有好几百人，且都是拥有各种各样背景，有着多样经历和工作经验的人。这个结果也在告诉我，不要再自我怀疑或怀疑他人，踏踏实实去积累，踏踏实实去成长，不要妄自菲薄，也不要急于求成，花开终有时。

一个看似不可能的"项目"已完成大半，考上这个结果可能并不是这次考研最终想赋予我的结果，而是在告诉我，努力尝试，坚持到底，你就一定走在更好自己的路上……

ranked first nationally in the second interview (including pre-interview) with a score of 286.65 points out of a total score of 300 points. It was undoubtedly the greatest affirmation of my experience, ideas and values formed over the years in CNOOD. I excelled among several hundred interviewees across China for the MBA pre-interview and second interview from all kinds of backgrounds with diversified life and work experience. This result also told me to stop questioning myself or others and grow steadily. Never underestimate yourself or be in a hurry for success. The flowers will blossom someday.

This seemingly impossible "project" has been largely completed. Maybe this result is not what this MBA entrance examination gives me eventually. Instead, it tells me that try hard and stick to it, and you will be on the way to a better self…

罗 蓉
Loreen Luo

管理学硕士，6年国际商务经验，3年高校大学生辅导员经历，年龄保密。对"人际交往"嗅觉敏锐，喜欢与人打交道，善于并热爱品研"情商管理"理论。通过生活和工作中与人的接触，体会到不论国别和年龄，不论教育与血缘关系，人心都是相通的，只有真心待人，才能获得他人的真心相待。

Loreen, with a master's degree in management, has 6 years' experience of international business and 3 years' experience of being a counselor in a college. Age is a secret. She has an acute sense in interpersonal interactions, love to associate with people and is fond of as well as good at studying EQ management theories. Through interactions with people in life and at work, she realizes that regardless of nationalities, ages, education backgrounds or blood relationships, people can feel each other's heart and that only by treating others with sincerity will one be treated with sincerity by others.

正视自己的内心

Face up to Your Inner Self

■ Billy Gu

2021年，我希望写的内容，能够在当稍有成绩时警醒自己，抑或在将来某一天陷入迷茫时帮助自己。

在这个瞬息万变的世界中，我们或多或少体会到这世界给我们带来的不安分、不公平，以至于使我们看不清自己的路该怎么走。是否要停下，抑或改变自己的前进的方向？回首以往，我时常会动摇自己定下的决心，当自己由于短暂的小成绩得到满足而忘却曾经坚定不移的信心，又回到自我放纵中的时候；当自己被可能不劳而获的利益所打动，想要放弃先前奋斗目标的时候；当自己在坚持一些目标而又得不到实际的反馈的时候，我必须提醒自己，请正视自己的内心，寻找到起初那份认真、那份执着、那份不求回报只求脚踏实地的热忱。

In 2021, I want to write something in the hope of guarding against conceit when I have achieved something or helping myself overcome confusion one day in the future.

In this rapidly changing world, we must have felt the restlessness and unfairness it brings us, to the extent that we can not see our way forward or make up our mind or whether we should pause for a while or change the direction. In the past, I often wavered in my determination. When I forgot all about my originally unshakable faith because of temporary tiny achievements and went back to self-indulgence, when I planned to give up my preset goals because of profits by other people's toil, and when I insisted on certain goals and received no feedback, I must remind myself to face my inner self and regain my previous earnestness, persistence and enthusiasm

　　类似的挣扎，今天一直存在，当人们摈弃自己的信仰、自己的目标，即使得到一些眼前的利益或者是自己所承受不住的好处时，却仍会不满足，仍然可能会感觉到沮丧。更不用说正在迷茫中，不知自己的路该怎么走的时候，至少在一段时间之内，我们是十分软弱的。假若我们此时的目标选择建立在某些错误的思想上，或者遵循某些现阶段无害的潮流，我们将会遭受更具毁灭性的试探。在这里，我有必要提醒自己，坚持起初的信仰，坚持自己的目标，不要在满足中自喜，亦不要在困难中放弃。

　　一方面，当我们有所成绩的时候，我们能否承受住这自以为莫大的喜悦，并且把这成绩当成我们对于信仰的坚持而感恩呢？从我自己出发，我发现我个人时常会站立不住，当得到些许成功的时候，我很容易放松，工作也好、健身也罢。我时常在达到一定的目标后容易陷在懒惰、享受

of keeping my feet on the ground and expecting nothing in return.

　　Similar struggles exist today. When we abandon our own beliefs and goals, or when we receive some immediate benefits or benefits that are irresistible to us, we won't be content and still feel frustrated, let alone confused and having no idea on how to proceed. For a while at least, we will be very weak. But if we choose to set our goals based on some wrong thoughts or go with some harmless flow now, we will be subjected to more destructive temptations. I need to remind myself here of sticking to my original faith and goals and not justifying myself for contentment or giving up in the face of difficulties.

　　When we have achieved something, can we bear this great joy in our own conceit and express gratitude to this achievement as our persistence on faith? Personally, I find that I can't bear it most of the time. When I have some success, I will easily slack off, at work and in

的试探中，而最终结果往往又会陷入困境。这是自我内心中堕落的一面，因此，我有必要时刻警醒自己，在任何时候都不要尝试将自己摆在易被试探的状态中，我们是经不起试探的，不要妄想靠着自己解决自己的软弱。一定要警醒自守，方可不陷入自我为是、自我骄傲的网罗。

另一方面，当我们遇到困难的时候，我们能否接受现实，接受结果并将此当作美好未来的基石呢？通常这都难以接受，我们很容易希望凡事都顺利，却无法理解为何会遭遇那些困难的境况。再次需要我们从起初的坚持或者信仰中得到帮助，才能把不喜欢的困难看成磨炼或者基石，引导自己回到正途，避免被陷在绝望的网罗中。

workout. When I achieve a certain goal, I will be easily tempted by laziness and enjoyment and eventually stuck in a difficult situation. This is a falling side of my inner self. Hence, it's necessary for me to always remind myself never to put myself in an easily tempted situation. We can't be tempted, and never try in vain to rely on ourselves to solve our own weakness. We must stay alert and hang on. Only in this way can we stay out of the snare of self-justification and self-pride.

When we have difficulties, can we accept them, embrace the present moment and take it as a foundation for a better future? Unusually it's difficult for us to accept them. We will easily hope that everything goes well and can't understand why we are in such a difficult situation. Once again I need help from my initial insistence or faith, so that I can see the unpleasant difficulties as discipline or building blocks in order to steer myself back to the right path and reduce the snare of despair which I am trapped in.

我发现无论是陷入享受、自我骄傲之中，还是陷入沮丧之类的情况时，出现试探的机会必定升高。只要我们变得软弱，试探必定变得更强，一旦我们察觉试探和我们自身的问题，常让我们陷入更深的绝望。我们会质问，一个曾经有坚定信仰和目标的人为何会有这种的思想？为何会渴望做这种的事呢？如此一来，我们就把试探当作是自己的问题。试探其实不是问题，屈服在试探之下才是问题的根本。

2021年，我要持续正视自己的内心，我所做的一切，其出发点是最初坚定的信仰和目标。此刻，我能理解我们董事长所说的平常心是何等的重要。我们的喜悦是建立在我们得到的回报，还是起初为了脚踏实地的热忱；我们的忧虑是来自得不到公平的对待，还是对自己没有尽到应尽的责任。举一些自己的例子：比如健身，我的出发点是为了健康，有持续的动力、清晰的思路、清醒的头脑，不是为了练成肌

I find that when I am caught up in enjoyment, self pride or frustration, the chances of temptation will surely rise. As long as we become weak, temptations will be stronger. Once we notice the temptations and our own problems, we will often plunge deeper into despair. We will question why a man who once had such strong beliefs and goals would have such thoughts and yearn for such things. As a result, we will take temptations as the problem. As a matter of fact, temptations are not the problem, and yielding to temptations is what the problem is.

In 2021, I will continue to face my inner self. Is everything I do meant for my previous firm belief and goal? At this moment I finally understand how important the peace of mind our Chairman proposed is. Is our joy built on what we get in return or the zeal of keeping on the ground? Is our anxiety derived from unfair treatment or unfulfilled responsibility? Take myself

肉男或者男模身材，从而得到别人的赞赏。又比如工作，我需要时刻认真努力地工作，是为了能在每一个任务中尽力做到踏实落地，能成就自己，造福团队；而不是为了得到回报，炫耀自己，得到众人瞩目的眼光。信仰亦是如此，是为了时刻归正自己，免得让自己陷入自负、欺骗、骄傲、嫉妒的网罗；而不是为了教导别人，让别人认为自己是敬虔的人，从中得到虚妄的满足。

我必须正视自己的内心。

for example. I work out for the purpose of health, a continuous driving force and a clear mind, instead of for becoming a muscle man or a male model physique and winning appreciation from others. I work earnestly to stand on solid ground in each task, build myself and the team, and thus do good to others, instead of receiving exceptional returns, glorifying myself and getting all the attention. So is faith, which is to correct yourself and stop yourself from plunging into the snare of self-justification, fraud, pride and envy, not to teach others, make yourself a pious man and get false satisfaction.

I must face my inner self.

顾天阳
Billy Gu

2010年正式加入CNOOD工作至今，现为高级客户经理，学历MBA。见证了CNOOD每一次起点，每一次奇迹的发生。从一般贸易到工程贸易，从工程贸易到项目采购中心，现在又在为公司成为真正的EPC工程公司而努力。相信：一切不是最好就没到最后。

Billy has been working at CNOOD since he joined the company in 2010. Now he is a senior account manager at CNOOD with an MBA degree. He has witnessed every starting point of CNOOD and every time a miracle has occurred. Having witnessed the transformation of CNOOD from a company focused on general trade to one engaged in engineering trade, and again to a project procurement center, now he is making efforts to help CNOOD become a true EPC company. He believes that it is not the end if everything is not the best.

当下每一天

Living Every Day of My Life

■ Chris Lee

常常和朋友们畅想起未来，也经常和同事领导们沟通起长远的规划。

往往不太能像朋友们那样目标明确，也难以像同事们规划清晰。

有时候，只好腼腆地笑着说：

我呢，就是过好今天，做好每一天。

有时项目上突然多了棘手的待处理事项。

有时客户集中发了几个着急的需求。

有时投标进度到了最后的递交时间。

多件事情，进度交织在一起。

难免有焦虑，也不免会着急。

I often envision the future with my friends and talk with my coworkers and leaders about long-term plans.

Most of the time I don't have well-defined goals like my friends or well-made plans like my coworkers.

Sometimes I can only respond with a bashful smile,

"I live my life to the fullest every day."

Sometimes there are suddenly a couple of tricky project problems to be resolved.

Sometimes customers send a couple of pressing requirements to be met.

Sometimes it's time to submit the final bid documents.

With so many tasks to be handled all at once,

It's hard not to feel anxious and worried.

头脑里在过着解决方案。
思绪在梳理着轻重缓急。

深呼吸几口气,打开水龙头打湿脸庞。

眼下最着急的事情是哪一件?
手头最有资源处理的是哪一环节?

或者,是太饿了,该去补充能量,回来再战。

一杯咖啡,几颗坚果,一盒水果,几只馄饨。
打开新闻,看看关注的那支足球队最新的趣事。

精力满满,脑海里也浮现了当下的件件事情。
一件一件事情来,做起来,做好它。

待处理事项清单,一条条地关闭。
客户的需求,一件件地回复。

沉下心来,又过了遍投标文件,稳稳地点击 Submit。

回去休息的路上,放起舒缓的轻音乐。
回想起这一天的时间,好像过去的一周、一个月、一年,都是今天的缩影。

停车,落锁,走在夜空下。

抬头,皓月当空,月朗星稀。

Finding solutions,
and clarifying priorities,

take a few deep breaths and wet my face with tap water.

Which is the most pressing task?
Which problem can be handled with the resources at hand?

Well, perhaps I am just too hungry. Go grab a bite and then continue.

A cup of coffee, several nuts, a fruit box and several wontons.

Turn on the news to learn about the latest news about my favourite football team.

Refreshed, I can't help but think of the tasks at hand.

Just tackle them one by one in perfection.

The to-do lists are closed one by one.
The customer requirements are replied.

Calm down, go through the bid documents again, and then click "Submit."

On my way home, I play some soothing music.

As I recall how I spent the day, it seems that today is the epitome of last week, last month and last year.

Park the car, lock it and walk under the starry sky.

Look up and see the bright moon and stars.

低头，路在脚下，坚实向前。　　　　　　Look down and march forward steadily.

做好眼前事。　　　　　　　　　　　　　Accomplish the current tasks.
珍惜每一天。　　　　　　　　　　　　　Cherish every day.
未来，就在一步步道路的那边。　　　　　March into the future to which the road leads.

李云龙
Chris Lee

中共党员，东华大学机械工程学院机械制造及其自动化硕士。加入施璐德 7 年。

Member of the communist Party of China, Master of Engineering in mechanical engineering and its automation from Donghua University, and member of CNOOD for 7 years.

少说太难，说我可以

Say "It's hard" less and "I can" more

■ Heather Zhang

2020年是极不平凡的一年。这一年，我们共同见证了诸多不曾有过的重大事件：有史以来最漫长也是最难熬的春节，疫情下无数逆行者的壮举，居家办公新模式的出现和适应以及国内国际供应链遭遇的巨大挑战。

我们每个人都是历史的见证者，也是历史的创造者。身处时代的大山之下，我们每个人即使渺小如尘埃，依旧选择守望相助，永不言弃。中国自古以来就有"一方有难，八方支援"的优良传统。面对疫情，公司上下团结一心，捐款捐物驰援灾区，为缅甸灾区献上爱心。春节后复工初期，面对道路封闭、人员隔离等突发情况，公司各个项目组充分发挥责任与担当，尽最大努力不惜成本如期完成项目的交付。海内存知己，天涯若比邻。海外项目部的同事面临更为严峻的疫情形势和身心压力，依然克服重重困难，坚守岗位，

The year 2020 was an extraordinary year. In the past year, we have witnessed many unprecedented events: the longest and the most difficult Spring Festival ever, the feats of countless heroes fighting against COVID-19, the emergence of and adaptation to the new homeworking mode, and the great challenges in domestic and international supply chains.

Each of us is a witness to and a creator of history. In the face of the times, each of us, even if small as dust, still chooses to help each other and never gives up. Since ancient times, China has forged a fine tradition of "trouble in one side, support in all directions." In response to the epidemic, the company united as one, donated funds and materials to help the disaster-hit areas and showed care for the disaster-hit areas in Myanmar. Despite road closure, personnel isolation and other situations in the beginning of work

默默付出，直到 2020 年 12 月底，在海外的同事们才陆陆续续凯旋并且零感染。我想为每一位平凡且伟大的同仁点赞！

经历这一年，自己又多了一份成熟和稳重。虽然还是会间断性陷入焦虑，但也会很快提醒自己"立刻投入行动，把事做成"。这样的自我鼓励、自我肯定，很有用。做项目管理，开发客户，最难是沟通：通过沟通把最有价值的 1~2 个差异点准确传递给合适的客户。所以做一个连接者，做一个读心者，做一个能把所有人整合在一起的人也是一件不容易的事情。在销售这条路上，自己还有很长一段路要走，唯有勤奋和坚持，不断学习、不断尝试、不断总结，才会有进步。

业精于勤荒于嬉，转眼已到 2021 年，给自己定个新的目标，要更积极开放，少说"太难"，说"我可以"。期待个人有新

resumption after the Spring Festival, our project teams had given full play to their responsibilities and tried our best to deliver the projects on time regardless of cost. A bosom friend afar brings a distant land near. Our coworkers in the Overseas Project Department were faced with physical and mental pressure under a more severe epidemic situation, and yet they overcame numerous difficulties, stuck to their posts and worked silently. It was not until the end of December that our overseas coworkers returned home triumphantly without a single case of infection. I am truly proud of every ordinary and great coworker!

Another year of life and work experience has made me more mature and stable. Although I may be anxious occasionally, I would immediately urge myself to "take actions now and get things done." Such self-encouragement and self-affirmation is quite helpful. The biggest challenge in project management and customer management is communication: accurately conveying the 1 or 2 most valuable differences to proper customers through communication. Therefore, it's not easy to work as a connector, a mind reader and a person to gather all others. I still have a long way to go on the path of marketing. Only with diligence, insistence, and constant learning, trying and summarization can progress be made.

Achievement is founded on diligence and wasted upon recklessness. In 2021, I have set a new goal for myself: be more

的成长，公司蒸蒸日上，每一位同事都能收获幸福、事业进步！

active and open, and say "It's hard" less and "I can" more. I look forward to new personal growth, business prosperity of the Company, and happiness and career progress for every coworker!

张霄燕
Heather Zhang

中共党员，上海对外经贸大学经济学硕士，于2014年4月加入施璐德。

Member of the Communist Party of China and Master of Economics from Shanghai University of International Business and Economics, joined CNOOD in April 2014.

2021 随 想

Random Thoughts in 2021

■ Danni Xu

新冠肺炎疫情的发展出乎意料，病毒没有国界，疫情不分种族。疫情在全球多点暴发并快速蔓延，至今仍未得到有效控制。由于我国对疫情管控严格、科学，个人防控意识强，我国的疫情已得到控制。

受新冠肺炎疫情全球肆虐的影响，2020年我们已签约项目的进展延迟，待签项目暂缓。在这一年的时间里，我们做出了一系列调整和改革，以稳定人心，共克时艰。在大家的努力下，缅甸项目、本溪项目相继进入收尾阶段，我们历经磨难而保持定力。与此同时，在新的大环境下，我们开始向国内市场进军，应对变局并开创新局。

The COVID-19 epidemic took an unexpected turn, now found all over the world regardless of border or race. The epidemic has broken out in many parts of the world and spread rapidly, and has yet to be effectively controlled.

Due to the worldwide spread of COVID-19, our projects signed in 2020 were postponed and projects to be signed were suspended. Over the past year, we have made adjustments and reforms to stabilize the team and overcome the challenges together. With our concerted efforts, the Myanmar Project and Benxi Project entered into the final stage successively. We have maintained our composure through trials and tribulations. In response to the new environment, we have started to enter into the Chinese mainland market to cope with the changes and break new ground.

2021年年初,公司出台了2021年主要工作计划指导性文件,涉及合伙人队伍建设、子公司业务发展、业务模式创新、平台建设加速、公司治理完善、对外宣传加强等方方面面。目前这些工作都在有条不紊地推进中。4月14日,公司更新发布了施璐德新版网站,更加直观地展示了公司的综合实力。

Earlier this year CNOOD issued the 2021 guidance document of main work plans on partner team building, business development of subsidiaries, innovative business model, accelerated platform building, improving corporate governance and increasing external publicity efforts. These projects are now being advanced orderly. On April 14, CNOOD launched the updated official website to showcase our comprehensive strength in a more intuitive manner.

从个人角度而言，这一年我经历了各种角色转变，有职能上的，也有方向上的。随着部门成员的加入，我感觉自己的责任更重了。以前一个人默默完成的事，现在有了可以商量的队友。孤独的工作，融入默契的团队协作，我觉得前方的路更宽广更清晰了。征途漫漫，唯有奋斗。不忘初心，方得始终。我希望在未来，自己能明白真正想要的是什么，并为此拥有一往无前的决心和永不言弃的毅力，不断充实和丰富自己，最终实现它。

Personally, I have undergone all kinds of role changes over the past year, functionally and directionally. With the addition of new members in the department, I feel a heavier responsibility on my shoulders. Things I used to do alone can now be discussed with my teammates. Working alone is now combined with teamwork. I can see a wider and clearer path ahead. To finish the long journey, we can only forge ahead. Only those who stay true to their original aspiration can accomplish it. I hope that I can figure out what I truly want and have the determination and perseverance to accomplish it by constantly enriching myself in the future.

徐丹妮
Danni Xu

2016年4月正式加入施璐德，成为公司投融资部的一名成员。渴望拥有吃喝玩乐的生活和充实的精神世界，并为此不懈努力。

Danni formally joined CNOOD in April 2016 and became a member of the investment and financing department. She longs to have an enjoyable material life and an affluent spiritual life and is making unremitting efforts to achieve these.

从 心 出 发

Start with the Heart

■ David Wang

"从心出发",这是我2020年9月8日第一天踏入施璐德公司,第一眼看到的、也是至今让我印象深刻的一句话。

在过去近十年的时间里,我在海外的时间较多。美国留学、欧洲工作的经历让我看到了世界上很美好的事物:人、自然景观、美食等等,发现、感知美好事物的同时,更拓宽了我的视野以及对世界的认知,也更加坚定了努力创造美好的冲动,那就是创造属于我的事业。

2020年9月加入施璐德至今,和Dennis有很多思想上的碰撞,很快我们在某些领域就找到了新的商机与项目切入点。和之前角色不同的是,我成了项目的主管,不光要做好业务端到端的设计、市场洞察、风险预计与把控,还要考虑业务的顶层设计,比如项目如何运作才可以给公司创造更多的价值,销售激励方案如何

"Start with the heart" is the first slogan that I saw on my first day to CNOOD on September 8, 2020, which impressed me most so far.

Over the past decade or so, I have spent most of my time overseas. While studying in the United States and working in Europe, I have seen such wonderful things as people, scenery and food in the world, which at the same time expanded my horizon and view of the world. These experiences have further planted a seed of creating something wonderful in my mind which is creating my own career.

Since my entry to CNOOD, I have had an extensive exchange of ideas with Dennis. Soon we have found new opportunities and project starting points in certain fields. Taking a different role from previous ones, I have now become a project owner, responsible for end-to-end business design, market survey,

才能刺激销售活力，团队搭建选择如何才能将成员各自优势转化为核心生产力，项目管理手段如何设计才能控制业务风险等。虽然压力在所难免，但我很享受当下的状态：真正地从内心出发，站在用户的角度去思考产品、体验与服务。虽然项目还在筹建中，我想我已经收获很多了。该产品、解决方案是否可以复制？是否可以触类旁通？这些思考与自我赋能让我提高很快。

risk prediction and control as well as top-level business design. How can the project work to create more value for the company? How can a sales incentive program stimulate sales activity? How can team building choices translate the team's strengths into core productivity? How to design the project management measures to control business risks? Though working under pressure inevitably, I enjoy what I am doing: really think with the heart about products, experiences and services from the users' point of view. The project is still under construction, but I have gained a lot. Can this product or solution be replicated? Can it relate to other projects? These reflections and self-empowerment have quickly improved myself.

虽然加入施璐德的时间并不长，但我坚信，在施璐德我可以做很多尝试。冥冥之中，在未来至少十年的时间里，施璐德的经历将会成为我人生中很精彩的一段旅途。

路在脚下，每一步都是双脚沾满泥闯出来的！加油！施璐德人！

Though not a veteran in CNOOD, I am convinced that I can make many more attempts here. For the next decade at least, the CNOOD experience will be a wonderful journey in my life.

Every step we have taken is filled with mud on the road! All members of CNOOD, keep fighting!

汪耘拓
David Wang

90后，浙江杭州人。毕业于美国伊利诺伊大学香槟分校，曾在华为公司欧洲区任职，现为施璐德亚洲有限公司业务合伙人。

A 1990s-born native of Hangzhou, Zhejiang Province, a graduate of University of Illinois at Urbana-Champaign, a former employee of Huawei Europe and a current business partner of CNOOD.

感于心 践于行

Embrace Warmth and Put it into Practice

■ Iris Tong

时光匆匆，光阴荏苒。自2021年1月至今，我已在施璐德实习和工作四个多月了。在领导的关心支持下，在同事们的悉心帮助指导下，我已初步了解和掌握了HR岗位的基本工作内容与方法。同时，我深刻地意识到，"纸上得来终觉浅，绝知此事要躬行"，一个人的知识和能力只有在实践中才能得以提高，理论应该与实践相结合。下面我想就自己在施璐德工作这段时间的两个印象深刻的事件进行一个小回顾。

1. 参与MWC上海展会

2021年2月23—25日，我跟其他三名同事一起参加了世界移动通信大会（Mobile World Congress, MWC）。世界移

How time flies! It has been four months since I joined CNOOD as an intern in January 2021. With the care and support from the leaders and the assistance and guidance from my coworkers, I have gained a preliminary understanding of the basic job requirements and working procedures of a HR specialist. Meanwhile, I have never felt so true about the saying that "what you have read remains shallow, and you have to practice it before you can know about it profoundly." One's knowledge and capability can only be improved in practice which should be guided by theory. Here is a review of two events which impressed me most over the past couple of months.

1. Attending the MWC

I attended the MWC, short for Mobile World Congress, with three other coworkers from February 23 to February

动通信大会是一年一度的行业大会，由移动通信亚洲大会发起，已经成为全球最具影响力的移动通信领域的展览会，由全球移动通信系统协会主办，最早于1995年在西班牙马德里举行。本次的展会主题为"和合共生"，重点关注智能连接，并聚焦于特定行业主题，包括5G连接、行业智联、人工智能和初创企业创新。此次，我们参与了一个围绕"5G终端，商业化与部署速度与疫情影响同时能够带来哪些商业机会"的研讨会。其中最精彩的部分是有关"5G带来哪些创新与改变"这个小问题，通过我自己的思考与研讨会的讨论，有如下四点来回答这个小问题：（1）终端的改变：一个连接人与社会的桥梁随着个人移动的信息终端，向5G、人工智能等的转变。终端的获取信息与运算能力未来提升。（2）追求美与个性化。例如，在游泳时候泳衣可以与泳镜之间联动，自己的泳姿与标准差异。（3）教育评估体系会发生变化：通过终端记录学习过程，学生甚至不需要带书与作业本。例如，AI算法可以算出对孩子来说适合做什么，不适合做什么，并且不需要期末考试。又如，面试官调取面试者的资料，就知道面试者适合于否。（4）工作效率更高，生活更简单。

25. Initiated by Mobile Asia Congress, this annual event has become the world's most influential mobile communication exhibition. Sponsored by the Global System for Mobile Communications Association (GSMA), it was first held in Madrid, Spain in 1995. Themed with Connected Impact, the MWC this year focused on intelligent connection as well as special issues such as 5G connection, industry intelligence, artificial intelligence and start-up innovation. During the MWC, we attended a seminar on what business opportunities 5G terminals, commercialization and deployment speed and the COVID-19 pandemic can bring about. The most fascinating part was the question on what innovations and changes 5G can bring about. Here is the answer from my reflections and discussions on the seminar: (1) Terminal changes: A mobile information terminal serves as a bridge that connect people with the community, and 5G can enhance the future information acquisition and computational capability of bandwidth, AI and other terminals. (2) Pursuit of beauty and personalization. For instance, the swimming suit can be connected with the swimming goggles during swimming to adjust the swimming strokes. (3) Changes in education evaluation system: By recording the learning process through the terminal, students do not need to bring books and exercises home. The AI algorithms can figure out what's appropriate for a child and what's not,

本次 MWC 展会使我受益匪浅，期望以后还会有更多的参与活动机会让自己更上一层楼。

2. TED 演讲大赛培训

2021 年 5 月 7—8 日，来自上海其军管理咨询中心的叶军老师给我们施璐德的同事带来了主题为"TED 演讲大赛"的专业培训。培训开始时，叶老师首先让我们在场的各位同事上台做简短的自我介绍。这里我们学到了"MTV 自我介绍法"，就是自我介绍中要包含并回答三个问题：（1）我是谁；（2）我有过什么成就；（3）我能提供什么价值。接下来依次回放录制的自我介绍小视频并指正同事们的小问题，例如，发言时手在整理衣服、双手交叉臂弯放在胸前、没有面对观众讲话等。

之后的课程中，叶老师又阐述了学好演讲的目的：（1）对个人的价值是培养严谨的逻辑性和训练打动观众的能力；（2）对公司的价值是让问题更快速地解决和让公司更高效地运转；（3）对社会的价值是传播有价值的观点。随后，我们学习到几点有关卓越演讲者的能力，分别为：专业知识、技巧呈现、内容设计、互动控场以及自信魅力。我还记忆犹新的是老师给同事们播放了一档名为《赢在中国》中有关选手争取创业投资的演讲环节，由此我学习到创业演讲的套路：（1）为什么能赚钱；（2）能赚多少钱；（3）为什么是我

and no final exam is required. Another example is interview data calling to see if the candidate is a good fit or not. (4) Higher working efficiency and simpler life.

Gaining a lot from this MWC, I hope to attend more exhibitions like this to take myself to the next level.

2. TED talks training

From May 7 to May 8, 2021, Mr. Ye from Shanghai Qijun Management Consulting Center gave CNOOD a training session on TED Talks. At the beginning of the training session, Mr. Ye invited us to make a brief self-introduction. Then he taught me the MTV self-introduction method: (1) me; (2) thing; (3) value. After that he replayed the self-introduction video and corrected our problems such as fixing our clothes with our hands as we spoke, crossing our arms in front of our chest and failing to look at the audience as we spoke.

With that, he elaborated the purposes of learning public speaking: (1) personally, it's to develop rigorous logical thinking and practice how to relate to the audience; (2) for the company, it's to resolve problems faster and run the company more effectively; (3) socially, it's to spread valuable viewpoints. Then we learned about the capabilities of an excellent public speaker, namely, professional knowledge, presentation skills, content design, interaction control, confidence and charisma. I was impressed by the

们;(4)能赚多长时间。

本次培训让我们收获颇丰,不仅从演讲的内容上让我们提升,还让我们领悟了更多的实际操作方法。

感于心 践于行

"路漫漫其远修兮,吾将上下而求索。"在施璐德HR岗位锻炼期间,不仅拉近了我与社会的距离,让我学习到很多知识,开拓了视野,我还有了成长的许多内心感悟,它会让我终身受用。我切身意识到,施璐德就像一个温暖的大家庭,我不会忘记在每次我有困惑向同事领导们请教时得到的悉心指导以及耐心友善的无私帮助,我会珍惜这份温暖和关怀,并一直铭记在心。感于心,践于行。在接下来的日子里,我将加倍珍惜,继续向优秀的前辈们学习,同时努力提升自己。

speech made by the contestants to win start-up funds in the show "Win in China" played by Mr. Ye. From the video I learned about the pattern of a startup speech: (1) why; (2) how; (3) who; (4) when.

This fruitful training session has provided us with not only related knowledge, but also practical operation methods.

Embrace Warmth and Put It into Practice

"The way ahead is long. I see no ending, yet high and low I'll search with my will unbending." The internship in CNOOD has not only brought me closer to the society, but also enriched my knowledge, expanded my horizon and inspired me for the rest of my life. I have come to realize that CNOOD is a big warm family. I will never forget how my coworkers and leaders have guided, helped me patiently and selflessly. I will always cherish such warmth and care, put it into practice, continue to learn from the excellent predecessors and strive to improve myself.

佟秋瞳
Iris Tong

95后,硕士研究生毕业。先后留学澳大利亚和新加坡。于2021年1月加入施璐德大家庭,作为一名职场新人,愿以踏实的态度迎接每一份挑战。

Born after 1995, a holder of master's degree, having studied in Australia and Singapore, joined CNOOD in January 2021, ready to embrace every challenge pragmatically.

感恩，再出发
Grateful and Starting off again

■ Johnson Shen

2020年，三十而立。

2020年是我在CNOOD度过的第7年。从稚嫩青涩到羽翼渐丰，很庆幸能够在这里成长和进步。

一直以来，人们喜欢给人生标识刻度，以此来衡量每个人生的进程和质量，我时常会思考，三十而立，其中的"立"究竟是什么？立身，立家，立业？然而，我更认可的，是找到自己立足在这个世界上的原则、规律。唯有如此，才能坦然面对生命中的一切。

回顾2020年，这是艰难的一年，随着世界各国疫情的暴发，大部分海外项目被迫暂停和延期，一些原先已经计划纳入2020年销售额的项目也被迫中止。可以说，这一年是公司艰难生存的一年。

The year 2020 marked my thirtieth birthday.

It was also my seventh anniversary in CNOOD. From a rookie to a fledgling, I feel fortunate to grow and progress here.

People have always loved to mark their lives to measure each milestone and the quality of life. I often ponder over the old saying that a man should be independent at the age of thirty. What does it mean by "being independent"? Cultivating self morality, starting a family or building a career? However, what I prefer and appreciate is finding the principles and rules to gain a foothold in this world. Only in this way can we calmly face everything in life.

The year 2020 was a tough year. With the outbreak of COVID-19 around the world, most overseas projects were suspended or postponed, and a handful of projects which had been included into

同样由于疫情影响，海外项目的竞争形势明显加剧，海外客户对于价格的敏感度变得更高，国外竞争企业也由于自身产能过剩，急需订单维持生计，因此海外的供应成本也极具下降，一些势在必得的项目却沦为价格战的牺牲品。

在不利的大环境下，重要的是心态和沉淀，调整和前行。只有经历过风雨的企业，才能在市场中站得更稳，走得更远。只有经历过磨炼的心灵，才能以更加饱满的姿态去迎接充满未知和希望的将来。

阿兰·德波顿在《哲学的慰藉》中写道，每一种挫折的核心都有着同样的基本构成，那就是主观愿望与严酷现实之间的冲突。而我们所要达到的智慧，就是要学习如何避免用我们对挫折的反应来加剧这个世界的顽固性。这种反应包括盛怒、自怜、焦虑、怨恨、自以为是和偏执。

一直以来，我都尽量让自己的心境处于一个比较稳定的状态。在处理纷繁的项目管理事宜时，我也时常会让自己静下来去思考，思考这个世界的一种"必然"和"秩序"。无论是一次次的艰难沟通，还是

the statement of sales were terminated. It was a year CNOOD was struggling to survive.

Affected by the epidemic, the overseas projects were faced with noticeably keener competition. Overseas customers were more sensitive to price. Our rivals overseas were in desperate need of orders to maintain their livelihood due to excessive productivity, greatly reducing the overseas supply costs. Hence, a few projects which we were determined to win were eventually reduced to victims of the price war.

In such an unfavourable environment, what matters most is mentality, accumulation, adjustment and progress. Only enterprises which have weathered the storms can gain a firmer foothold in the market and go further. Only a tempered mind can embrace the unknown and promising future in a better state.

Alain De Botton writes in *The Consolation of Philosophy* that at the core of every frustration is the same basic component, a conflict between desire and harsh reality. And the wisdom we need to achieve is to learn how not to exacerbate the world's obstinacy with our reactions to setbacks. Such reactions include rage, self-pity, anxiety, resentment, self-righteousness and paranoid.

I have always tried to maintain a steady mind. While handling complicated project management matters, I often settle down and think about the "inevitability" and "order" of the world.

多少个日日夜夜的不断修改，所付出的一切，都是源于内心的一种坚定信念。

2021年新年伊始，我又接受了一项新的挑战，兼任董事长助理一职。角色转变让我意识到需要不断提升视野和思维的高度。最近几个月来，"在路上"成为我的工作常态。跟随董事长不断进行战略业务开拓、方案谈判、事项规划，每分每秒都充满着未知和挑战，身体的每一个细胞都蕴藏着能量和热情。我感受到肩上沉甸甸的责任，也将一直全力以赴。

在这纷纷扰扰的世界，生活给你很多充满随心所欲的幻想。直到最后，我们终于恍然大悟，总有一些东西，值得让我们热爱，值得经历，值得期待。

三十而立，梦在心里，路在脚下。感恩，再出发。

Be it tough communication time and again or repeated revision for many days and nights, such endeavor comes from a firm belief.

At the beginning of this year, I accepted a new challenge by serving as the assistant to the Chairman concurrently. Such a role transition made me realize the need to constantly enhance the level of vision and thinking. Over the past couple months, I have been "on the road." Following the Chairman to constantly make strategic business expansion, negotiate plans and draw up project plans. Every second is unknown and challenging, and every cell in my body bursts out of energy and enthusiasm. With such a heavy responsibility on my shoulders, I will always do my best.

In this chaotic world, life gives you a lot of free fantasy. Finally, we will understand that there are things worthy of our devotion, experience and expectation.

At the age of thirty, I am grateful and starting off again towards my dream.

沈佳祺
Johnson Shen

所有的相遇，都是久别重逢。不知不觉在CNOOD已经七年多了。在这样一个关怀他人、提升自我的集体中，始终能让自己充满正能量。走遍世界的角落，带着自由而无用的灵魂。

Every occasion of encounter is a reunion after a long separation. I have been working at CNOOD for more than seven years before I know it. I am always filled with positive energy in such a mutually caring and self-promoting organization. With a free and useless soul, I'm adventuring to every corner of the world.

好 久 不 见

It's been a long time

■ Louise Ju

一、我心中的 CNOOD

1. 自由空间

对于老池和 Fay，我们从来都不是员工，而是他们最信任的合作伙伴。在 CNOOD，没有形式上的"官僚主义"，每个人都可以"做主"，都是"自己项目的老板"，很少有公司可以做到这样（至少在我看来每天讲着"垂直化、扁平化、简约化管理"的公司没有做到）。CNOOD 不会以任何一种形式约束大家，只是作为大家聚集的平台，尽可能地给予每个人充分的空间，你可以尽情地发挥和展示个人能力和创新想法，CNOOD 会帮助你成长、进步、积累财富。

2. 乐于分享

刚毕业的你最担心的就是从校园到职场身份转换，可能需要一个"师父"帮助

CNOOD in My Heart

1. Free space

For Dennis and Fay, we are not the employees. We are the partners who they most trust. There is no formal "bureaucracy" in CNOOD. Everyone can make their own decisions and be the boss of their own project. Few companies can be like this. (Many companies talking about "vertical, flat, simplified management" all the time fail to do so.) CNOOD won't restrain us in any form, It just serves enough space to everyone as a platform, where you can develop and showcase your abilities and innovative ideas. CNOOD will help you to grow, develop and accumulate wealth.

2. Enjoy sharing

From the campus to the company, the identity change worried me a lot when

你或指导你完成工作。但在 CNOOD 你永远不用担心自己是个"新人"。因为你会有几百位"师父",他们都是行业内的佼佼者,遍布中国各个城市,甚至全世界很多国家。这得益于 CNOOD 独特的合伙人制度和老池的"共同利益论"。你随时可以提问、咨询,不用担心你的问题是不是有点幼稚,因为他们永远会不厌其烦地解答你的问题,提出建议,并尽可能地提供更多的帮助。在 CNOOD,大家从不吝啬分享。只要他们知道的都会告诉你,如果他们不知道的,也会想办法告诉你。

I just graduated. At that time I hoped I could get a "master" to help me out and guide me to complete the work. But in CNOOD you never have to worry if you are a "newcomer," because you will have hundreds of "masters" who are the best in their field from all over the world, which benefits from the unique partner system and the theory of common interests of Dennis. You can always ask questions and consult without worrying about whether your question is a little childish, because they will never be tired of answering your questions, offering advice and helping you as much as possible. CNOOD is always generous on sharing. They'll tell you everything they know, and if they don't know, they'll find an answer for you.

3. 有爱的家

很多老板和员工只是雇主和雇员的关系，维系关系的因素只有劳动和钱，但CNOOD能给予每个人的不仅仅是银行卡上的数字。记得电影《西虹市首富》里有句台词"金钱是冰冷的，爱人的手才是温暖的"。所以与工作相比，我觉得更有意义的是CNOOD见证了很多人从青涩的学生变成职场精英、从单身到美好的恋爱，再到步入幸福的婚姻、生儿育女并为人父母，甚至有些小伙伴家里遭遇不幸，也有CNOOD的陪伴和支持。这每一件对于我们都是人生"大事"，或喜或悲，但CNOOD一直都在。与其说我们的一生可以在CNOOD度过，不如说CNOOD陪伴我们走过一生。CNOOD让我觉得这个世界是有温度的，不是冰冷的。CNOOD让我觉得无论是身在异乡，还是远在千里，都有归宿。

二、一些小建议

1. 管理理念

八年前，很多人不理解CNOOD，当时北京办公室的老崔总一直希望池总步伐可以慢一点，用传统公司的管理理念运营公司。但八年后的今天再回首，看着市场

3. Home with Love

Most of the relationship between the boss and the employee is just the relationship between the employer and the employee: the work and money are the only things that they are thinking about. However, CNOOD gives us more than the number in our bank card. There is a line I remember in the movie *Hello Mr. Billionaire*: "Money is cold, but the hand of a lover is warm". So I think what is more significant than work is that CNOOD has seen a lot of people grow from a young student to a professional elite, from single to marriage and having children and being a parent. Even some co-workers suffered from family misfortunes and had CNOOD's support. All those things are important in our lives, whether we like them or not, and CNOOD always stays with us. Instead of saying that we spend all our lifetime at CNOOD, I would rather say that it's CNOOD accompanying us all the time. CNOOD makes me think that the world is warm, not that cold. CNOOD makes me feel like I have a home to back, whether I am in a foreign country or thousands of miles away.

A Few Tips

1. Management concepts

Eight years ago, many people didn't understand CNOOD or Dennis.Mr Cui, the boss of Beijing office, has been

上的企业纷纷转型、国企全面改制，连学校里的教学案例都在更新迭代地推送创新管理、扁平化运营和合伙人制度的学习。你就不得不佩服和理解老池曾经提出的现代化管理理念是多么的超前和成功！当时 Fay 做过一版工作手册，CNOOD 现在可能早已更新迭代很多版本了。但最初那个 1.0 版本对现在的我做任何工作依旧很有用。可能很多年以后我们都不会记得手册里面的具体内容了，但我想 Fay 教给我们的本就不是按部就班地参照手册执行，而是培养我们缜密的逻辑思维和清晰的条理去思考和解决问题的能力。

2. 不断学习

我是从一所普通本科院校毕业的，学校不是 211 和 985 院校。但因为老池和 Fay 的鼓励以及 CNOOD 的学习氛围，让我决定继续进修学习，最后成功考入中央财经大学攻读硕士学位。当然还有个原因是当时我觉得自己跟不上 CNOOD 的发展步伐，我很幸运有这样的机会弥补自身不足。随着不断学习、成长，我看到的很多东西都变得不一样了，原来只要向前再迈进一步，视野就会变得如此宽阔。就在前几天，我还和父母说，我有继续读博的

hoping Dennis could slow down the pace of development and run the company with the traditional company management philosophy. But eight years later, we are looking at the many enterprise transformation(s) in the market and the overall restructuring of state-owned enterprises, and even the teaching cases in schools are all in the process of updating to study innovation management, flat operation and the partnership system. You have to admire and understand how advanced and successful Dennis's modern management concept is! Faylee developed a work manual which may have been updated many times by now. But the original version is still useful to me for any work. We may not remember the details of the work manual for years to come, but I think what Faylee is trying to teach us is not a step-by-step guide, but the way to use clear organization and careful logical thinking to solve problems and complete the work.

2. Keep learning

I was a common undergraduate, not even from a Project 211 or 985 university. Thanks to the encouragement of Dennis and Faylee and the learning atmosphere of CNOOD, I decided to continue studying. Finally I was admitted to graduate school at Central University of Finance and Economics. Of course, The main reason was that I couldn't follow up with the development of CNOOD at that time, but I am so lucky that I had the opportunity

想法，现在也正在准备发表文章。虽然不一定会成功，但我不怕，因为我知道和失败相比，那种努力争取过的勇气更难得可贵。学习和工作都是一样的，不是吗？

3. 时间管理

CNOOD 的每一位小伙伴都是经过层层筛选的优秀人才，大家各有所长，并胸怀大志。可能短期内没有实现心中所向，请不要着急。因为任何事都是需要沉淀且有周期性的，尤其是在侧重项目为主的公司。你可能会集中一段时间很忙，又有一段时间清闲，忙的时候会让你学习到很多新知识，进步飞速；清闲的时候是留给大家休息和自我调整，要学会利用好这段时间充实自己。你只管努力就好，领导会看得见、客户会看得见、伙伴们会看得见、CNOOD 会看得见、时间也会看得见。

4. 成本管控

"家里日子要过好，就不要乱花钱，虽然父母从不亏待我们，但我们也要有节制的，把钱花到刀刃上。"这是长辈们常

to make up for it and to learn more after working. As you continue to learn and grow, many of the things you see become different, because your vision will become so much wider if you move just one more step. Just the other day I told my parents that I had the idea of continuing to Ph. D. and now I am preparing to publish essays for it. It may not work out, but I'm not afraid, because I know that the kind of courage to fight for something is more valuable than success. Study and work are the same. Isn't it?

3. Time management

Everyone at CNOOD is admitted through the screening of excellent talent; they have their own strengths and ambitions. Don't worry if you don't get what you want in the short term. Because everything has to be precipitated and is periodic. Especially since we are a project-oriented company, you may be very busy for a concentrated period of time and then have a period of leisure. Busy time will let you learn a lot of new knowledge and make rapid progress. Leisure time is reserved for rest and self-adjustment. Learn to use this time to enrich yourself. You just have to work hard. The leader will see, the customer will see; the partners will see; the CNOOD will see; the time will see.

4. Cost control

"If we want a good life at home, we should not spend money indiscriminately. Although our parents never treat us badly,

说的话，我觉得同样适用于我们工作中。比如：（1）供应商的筛选除综合实力、资质、人员等符合合作要求外，还要做同级三方比价，挑选最优价格，控制采购预算不要超支。（2）生产过程中，在保质保量的前提下，要避免人为因素增加的犯错成本，从而产生经济损失，如信息的沟通和传递。（3）与客户、供应商和相关合作方明确责任范围。（4）风险前置，多向他人请教经验内容易出错的关键因素节点，提前做好防控预案，订船时间、交货时间都要尽可能的留出空余。（5）注重团队合作，分工明确。（6）出差和接待的费用要尽可能控制和节约，避免不必要的开销和浪费。有的时候8元的啤酒比800元的红酒更好喝，20元的饺子比2 000元的西餐更好吃，因为用心待人才是最重要的。

we have to be restrained and spend the money on the blade." That's what the elders say, and I think it also applies to our work. For example: (1) In the selection of suppliers, in addition to looking at comprehensive strength, qualifications, personnel and other requirements for cooperation, we should also do a tripartite price comparison in the same class, pick the best price, and control the purchase budget without overspending. (2) In the course of production, on the premise of quality and quantity, we must avoid the increased costs of human error that lead to economic losses, such as errors in communication and transmission of information. (3) Clarify the scope of responsibility of customers, suppliers and relevant partners. (4) Risk leading, ask others for advice on the error-prone key elements from experience, make the prevention and control plan in advance, and leave as much spare time as possible for booking and delivery. (5) Pay attention to teamwork and clear the division of labor. (6) The cost of travelling and reception must be controlled and saved as much as possible. Avoid unnecessary overhead and waste. Sometimes, $8 beer is better than $800 wine, and $20 dumplings are better than a $2 000 western meal, because it is most important to treat people with heart.

5. 客户开发

中国很大，世界也很大。CNOOD一直在保护大家，但小燕子终究有一天要长大。每一位小伙伴都要有自我开发客户

5. Customer development

China is big, and so is the world. CNOOD has always been protecting us, but eventually the swallows will have to grow up.

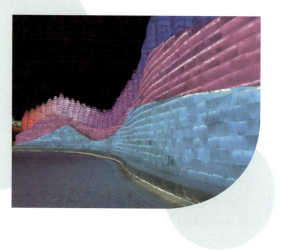

的能力。无论是线上平台还是线下资源整合。如果你有好点子、好创意、好项目，只要你提出来，相信老池和Fay一定会100%支持你，CNOOD也会是你们强有力的后盾。如果这是一次自我创业，那你们的起步点已经在CNOOD的平台之上了。

Every co-worker should have the ability to develop customers independently. Whether it is online or offline resource integration, if you have a good idea and a good project, as long as you put forward, I believe Dennis and Faylee will 100% support you, and CNOOD will also be your strong backing. If this is a start-up, you're already starting on top of the CNOOD platform.

6. 学会珍惜

我对CNOOD有很特殊的感情，从最初的合作关系到后来大家接纳我成为一家人，再到后来我去读书，就像是和CNOOD谈了一场恋爱。CNOOD帮助我成长、进步、开拓眼界，在CNOOD我结交了很多好朋友，有非常多美好的回忆。CNOOD真的给予我太多太多，就是这样有温度的公司，依旧在温暖千里以外的我，更何况是近在咫尺的你。真心希望所有的小伙伴们要懂得珍惜，学会感恩，不

6. Learn to cherish

I have a very special feeling for CNOOD. From the initial relationship of cooperation to later its acceptance of me as family, then to my going to school, I feel like falling in love with CNOOD. CNOOD has helped me grow, improve and broaden my horizons. I have made many good friends at CNOOD and has many good memories. CNOOD has really given me too much. It is such a warm company that still warms

负所望。同 CNOOD 一起乘风破浪、披荆斩棘，看遍万里山河，共享万里空晴。

最后，祝好！祝瘦！祝开心！祝美丽！祝发财！祝所有美好的人和事都在 CNOOD！

me although I'm a thousand kilometers away, not to mention you who are close by. I really hope everyone can cherish the present, learn to be grateful and live up to expectations. Along with the CNOOD, let's ride the waves, blaze the trail, see all the mountains and rivers, and then enjoy the sunshine.

Finally, best wishes! To thinness! Have Fun! Be beautiful! Good Luck! Wish all the good things and people are at CNOOD!

鞠 璐
Louise Ju

汉族，中共党员，1990 年出生，黑龙江人。2016 届中央财经大学工商管理（金融管理方向）硕士。性格直爽，喜欢旅游、看书、打羽毛球。

Ethnic Han, member of the Communist Party of China, born in Heilongjiang in 1990, 2016 graduate of Central University of Finance and Economics with a master's degree in business administration (financial management), lover of traveling, reading and badminton.

巴拿马之行

A Trip to Panama

■ Richard Cheng

2018年，我们与中国港湾工程有限公司签署了巴拿马阿马多尔邮轮码头工程分包合同，经过国内紧密的深化设计以及加工，我同Mary在2019年2月17日（农历正月十三），打了一个"飞的"前往巴拿马，进行前场的对接以及施工准备工作。

这是我第一次前往纬度如此之低又常年高温的地方，势必要一睹巴拿马运河的"一夫当关，万夫莫开"的气势（虽然最终一次也没有去）。

由于身体较胖，在巴拿马这高温、高湿的地方，一开始明显吃不消，从酒店出来，没走几步路，全身已经湿透，皮肤整天都有一种黏糊糊的感觉，这种状况，一直持续了两周。

项目坐落在巴拿马运河汇入太平洋的入口处，站在屋顶上，能够看到著名的巴

In 2018, CNOOD entered into a subcontract contract on Amador Cruise Terminal Project in Panama with China Harbour Engineering Co., Ltd. After intense detailed design and processing in China, Mary Dai and I flew to Panama on February 17, 2019 (the thirteenth day of the first lunar month) for preliminary job connection and construction preparation.

It was my first trip to such low latitudes with high temperatures throughout the year. I was determined to catch a glimpse of the imposing narrow pass of the Panama Canal, but I didn't go there eventually.

With a plump body, I could barely stand the high temperature and high humidity of Panama. Just a few steps from the hotel, I was wet through and felt sticky all day long. This went on for two weeks.

The project is located at the estuary of the Panama Canal flowing into the

拿马大桥。每天日落时分，华灯初上，将运河以及巴拿马大桥装饰的异常明亮与夺目；巴拿马的雨季，雨水如同女孩的脾气，从来不和你打招呼，哗的一下就倾盆而下，这也给驻守海外的工程人带来了烦恼，给施工进度陡增了不少难度。

巴拿马国土面积不足75万平方千米，人口不足450万，却是中美洲地区旅游最旺的国家。无论是工作日还是非工作日，巴拿马的古街上都是游客，戴着来自中国义乌的巴拿马传统服饰——巴拿马草帽，来一杯莫吉托，你便是整条街上最靓的仔。

Pacific Ocean. Standing on the rooftop, we could see the famous Panama Bridge. When the evening lights were lit at sunset every day, the Panama Canal and the Panama Bridge would be dazzling bright. The rainy season of Panama was like girls throwing a fit. You could never tell when it would come. The downpour also brought trouble to the engineers stationed overseas, increasing difficulties to the construction progress.

Despite a land area of less than 750,000 square kilometers and a population of less than 4.5 million, Panama is the most visited country in Central America. You could see the ancient streets of Panama packed with tourists wearing a Panama hat manufactured in the Chinese town of Yiwu on both weekdays and weekends. Grabbing a cup of Mojito, and you would be the most gorgeous guy in the street.

2020年10月，伴随着第一根钢柱的起吊，我们也结束了相对闲暇的生活，转成战斗模式。团队成员也陆续到位，美丽的阿马多尔，天气也变得火辣，空气也不再是那么香甜。晚间的闲逛，也成了考察当地施工的做法，为后面的施工进行准备，这也成了巴拿马邮轮码头项目能够较为顺利执行的一个侧面佐证。

In October 2020, our relatively leisure mode shifted to the battle mode with the hoisting of the first steel column. Our team members arrived in Panama successively. The beautiful Amador became scorchingly hot, and the air was not that sweet. The evening strolls turned into inspections of local construction methods to prepare for subsequent construction. It was also a proof of the successful execution of the Amador Cruise Terminal Project in Panama.

一切的付出都是值得的，当游轮码头航站楼主体以及通廊主体结构安装结束，我们站在码头上，看着对岸的巴拿马城，巴拿马城的游客们也在看着我们。也许他们会说："看，那边的工程做得好快，一天一个样的阿马多尔游轮码头，在不久的将来，游轮将靠在那里，载着我们走向深海。"

新冠肺炎疫情席卷了整个世界，巴拿马也未能幸免，国际航班也逐渐停航，远在巴拿马的我们，唯有加强自身的管理，减少被感染的可能。在炎热的天气里，一切以安全第一，我们调整工作时间，不与当地工人接触，戴着口罩进行施工。一次性医用口罩按规定可以带4个小时，但是在这炎热的天气下施工，口罩没一会便湿透了，所以每个人身上都带着好几个口罩，准备随时替换。

疫情不可怕，可怕的是无限期的居家隔离，充满孤独感，看着国内逐渐缓解的疫情，同胞们可以在大空下自由地呼吸，我们远在海外，也为祖国政府的管理方法与效率感到自豪。反观施工当地政府的管理方式，大街上人们戴口罩形式化地只遮住嘴，我们为当地疫情感到担忧。

All hard work paid off. When the main body of the cruise terminal and the main structure of the corridor were installed, we could see the Panama City across the river and the tourists looking at us in the terminal. They might say, "Look. The construction over there is fast. The Amador Cruise Terminal gains a new look everyday. Soon the cruises will berth there and take us to the depth of the sea."

The COVID-19 epidemic swept across the world. Panama was no exception to the pandemic. As the international flights were gradually grounded in Panama, we could only reduce the possibility of infection by strengthening body building. In hot weather, safety came first. We adjusted the working hours, stayed away from local workers, and carried out construction with a face mask. Disposable surgical masks were allowed to be worn for only four hours. However, the hot weather wet the masks after a short while. Hence, everyone took several masks with them for replacement.

The pandemic itself wasn't so horrifying as the endless home quarantine and loneliness. When we learned that the pandemic in China was kept under control and the Chinese people could breathe freely outdoors, we were proud of the Chinese government's management and efficiency. Yet we were sad to see the sloppy management of the Panamanian government, with people wearing masks that only cover their months in the streets.

曾经听过一句话"出国才知道祖国的伟大",一场疫情,让我们这些身处海外工程人才真正感到祖国的强大,祖国人民的高素质。在这场全球性突发公共卫生事件中,只有中国率先走出,最先开始复工复产。

春节临近,巴拿马城陆续出现一些新冠肺炎感染者。原先预定的年夜饭被迫取消,身边的战友们都有大半年没有回家,春节前回去已是不可能,每个人都希望能够吃到热腾腾的饺子,在一起喝一杯。

We heard that only when you go abroad will you know the greatness of your motherland. This pandemic allowed us overseas construction workers to truly feel the greatness of our motherland and the high quality of our countrymen. China was the first country to keep this pandemic under control and start work and production resumption.

As the Spring Festival approached, Panama City was seeing some COVID-19 infection cases. The scheduled dinner on the eve of Spring Festival had to be canceled. Our co-workers hadn't been home for more than half a year, yet it was impossible to return home before the Spring Festival. Everyone expected to have some hot dumplings and a good drink.

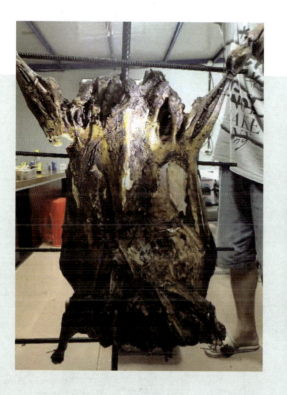

最终我们选择了一场不一样的年夜饭：一起烧烤。从农场主那里买了四只羊，大家一起吃烤全羊。大家也希望旺盛的篝火能够赶走疫情，期待来年的生活也是如此旺盛，项目早日完工，早日踏上回家的路！

过完2021年的春节，由于秘鲁市场有一些新的项目机会，便前往了美洲华人最多的国家——秘鲁。这是我第三次去秘鲁，一落地，秘鲁就宣布实施为期4个月的战时管理，关闭国际航班，我也开启了4个月的居家隔离生活。

Eventually we chose to have a unique barbecue dinner on the eve of Spring Festival. Four sheep were bought from a farmer, and we had roast whole sheep. We hoped that the bonfire could drive away the pandemic and bring prosperity next year. It's also hoped that the project could be completed as soon as possible, so that we could get home as soon as possible.

After the 2021 Spring Festival, I headed to Peru, the country with the most overseas Chinese in the Americas, for some new project opportunities there. The moment I landed on my third trip there, Peru started a 4-month wartime management period. The international flights were closed, and I began a 4-month home quarantine life.

程 杰
Richard Cheng

本科毕业于辽宁科技大学材料成型及控制工程专业，硕士毕业于上海大学冶金系，2017年加入施璐德亚洲有限公司，目前在业务发展部。

He received his bachelor's degree in material forming and control engineering from University of Science and Technology Liaoning and his master's degree in metallurgy from Shanghai University. He joined CNOOD in 2017 and is now working in Business Development Department.

2020 年的"幸运"

The "Fortunes" in 2020

■ Tommy Chen

梦想就像火苗，它能变成熊熊烈火，给人无限能量，也可能渐渐熄灭，让人感到迷茫从而迷失前进的方向。对于心中有着梦想与激情的人来说，每个人都是成功的。拥有梦想很容易，但缺乏指引的梦想始终是单薄且毫无生机的。身为追梦人的我们，能够在自己梦想的道路上获得指引并逐渐成长是一件非常幸运的事。一个人的成长来自多个方面，或许是成功人士的引领示范，或许是偶像榜样的模范力量，或许是亲人朋友的殷切期待，或许是不满现状的命运抗争。已经过去的 2020 年给所有人都留下了不平凡的一页，当中有坎坷有曲折，有辛酸有泪水，这一年的的确确发生了太多的不寻常，对我来说，这一年既是坎坷又是幸运的。

2020 年 3 月底，国内疫情状况趋于好转，武汉即将迎来解封，但此时的海外

Dreams are like flames which can turn into a blazing fire to give one infinite energy or die out to make one feel lost and lose his/her way. For those who harbour dreams and passion, everyone is successful. It's easy to have dreams, but dreams without guidance are inadequate and lifeless. As dream chasers, we are quite fortunate to obtain guidance on the path towards our dreams. The growth of an individual can be inspired by the guidance of successful people, the modeling of idols, the eager expectations of family members and friends, or the fight against destiny because of dissatisfaction about the status quo. The newly ended 2020 marks an extraordinary page in the book of life for everyone, filled with ups and downs and bitter tears. It's indeed an extraordinary year. For me, it's a rough yet fortunate year.

Last March, China's epidemic situation was improving, and Wuhan was about to

却陷入了疫情笼罩的阴云,远在英国的我内心充满着焦虑与不安,每天宅在宿舍的日子对我的精神无疑是一个莫大的考验。几番等待与周折过后,我终于在7月初踏上了回家的路。飞机落地的一瞬间,压抑在我心中的焦虑和恐惧一扫而光,我永远也忘不了那一天。7月4日,深圳宝安机场,下午1点30分左右,那天的深圳气温高达37度,无比闷热……我亲眼看到了身着防护服整装待命的医生、护士、警察、机场和酒店的防疫工作人员和保安。从飞机落地到酒店隔离,每个环节都有他们耐心和细心的指引。烈日炎炎,无比湿热的环境中,每个人都清楚那套密闭的防护服下承载了什么,但他们没有丝毫的怨言与懈怠。自从疫情出现以来,他们枕戈待旦,一刻都没有放松过警惕,用勇敢和无私坚守在国家最前沿的防线上。

lift the lockdown. The other countries, however, were shrouded by the epidemic. Stuck in the U.K., I felt anxious and insecure. Staying in the dormitory everyday was undoubtedly a major test for me. After months of waiting and a lot of trouble, I finally headed for home in early July. The moment the plane landed, my anxiety and horror cleared off. I would never forget that day. It was July 4 around 1:30 p.m. at Shenzhen Bao'an Airport. It was 37 degrees Celsius, stiflingly hot … I saw the doctors, nurses and policemen in protective garment as well as epidemic control staff and security officers of the airport and hotels, ready to serve. From plane landing to hotel quarantine, each step was taken with patience and thoughtful guidance. Everyone was aware of what it meant to work in the protective garment on such a hot and humid day, yet none of them complained or slacked off. Since the outbreak of the epidemic, they

在酒店隔离时网络不好，每天的娱乐只能依赖电视，记得当时疫情的防控仍在继续，祖国的南方又遭遇了洪水，隔着屏幕，我看到最多的就是和洪水战斗的解放军战士们。他们不分昼夜地奋战在灾区，因为国家和人民需要，他们就会奋不顾身。2020年，我已经被这些可爱的人感动了太多太多次。正是这一群默默无私奉献的人，我们才得以挺过当下这个特殊时期，在他们身上，我看到的是一种坚定而神圣的使命感和责任感，这种使命感与责任感也刷新了我对自己生活态度的认知。我们的人生同样需要赋予使命和责任，通过做有意义的事情，摆脱平庸。对自己的人生做到尽心尽责，不辜负自己内心所期，就是我们对自己最大的馈赠。回到祖国的那一刻，我觉得自己是幸运的，不仅仅是回家带来的安全感，更多的是收获了一种对人生态度的升华，它将永远成为我的精神财富，不断指引我成长，时刻带给我希望。

have never relaxed their vigilance and have stood on the front line of defense with courage and selflessness.

Due to poor internet access in the quarantine hotel room, I could only find entertainment on TV every day. While prevention and control of the epidemic continued, south China was hit by floods. On the screen I saw PLA soldiers fighting against the floods, working day and night in the flood-hit areas. When the country and people need them, they make their contribution with scant regard for their own safety. In 2020, I was touched by these lovely people for numerous times. It's this group of selfless and dedicated people that we tide over this special time. From them I saw a strong and sacred sense of purpose and responsibility which refreshed my perception of my own attitude to life. We also need to give purpose and responsibility to our lives. By doing something meaningful, we can escape mediocrity. Being responsible for our lives and living up to our own expectations is the greatest gift we can give to our lives. The moment I came back to China, I felt fortunate, not only for the sense of safety, but also for a sublimed attitude towards life. It will always be my spiritual wealth, constantly guiding my growth and bringing me hope.

2020年9月,我的人生状态迎来了一次全新的转变,结束了几年的海外大学生活步入职场。从加入施璐德这个大家庭开始,我的人生进入一种新的模式。与我脑海里固有对职场的理解不同,施璐德奉行着一种独特的文化理念。在公司,大家相互关心、创造开心,同事间互相尊重、以诚相待,共同创造了一种既高效又放松的工作环境。

在施璐德大家庭里,每一位成员各有所长,每个人都拥有独特的优势,却那么平易近人,由内而外,丝毫没有任何的骄躁之气,踏实笃定的平和心和进取心在这里被体现得淋漓尽致。入职以来,很大程度上得益于所处的环境,我有幸一直都在发现自己身上存在的不足。在我眼中,同事们每时每刻都在我周围扮演着榜样的角色,工作中的每一天里,他们的勤奋、踏实、坚持、乐观,时时刻刻都在给予我新的自省和自悟,与他们相处,我总是能够发掘出新的成长,这一点在职场中并不常见。能够身处这个大家庭之中,我觉得自己是非常幸运的。

In September 2020, my life took a whole new turn. After years of college life overseas, I started my career life and initiated a new lifestyle after joining the CNOOD family. Different from my stereotyped perception of a workplace, CNOOD upholds a unique cultural concept. All members care about, respect and trust each other, working together to create happiness and an efficient and relaxing working environment.

Each member of CNOOD has his/her expertise and unique strength, and at the same time, is approachable without the slightest trace of arrogance or rashness. The steadfast and peaceful mind and enterprising spirit are reflected incisively and vividly here. Since my entry into the big family, I have been fortunate to constantly find my shortcomings, which is to a large extent attributed to the environment I'm in. For me, my co-workers have served as role models on an ongoing basis. Their diligence, steadiness, perseverance and optimism at work have given me new reflections and insights all the time. Getting along with them, I can always explore new growth, which is uncommon in many workplaces. Therefore, I feel quite fortunate to be part of the CNOOD family.

茫茫人海中，我们每个人生来也是与众不同的，只要心中有梦，眼中有光，走到哪里都会收获幸运。每个人都拥有着自己的小幸运，当我们发现它，拥抱它，并最终收获这些幸运给我们的馈赠时，我们就是最幸运的。2020年，我为自己收获了追梦路上如此之多的财富而感到幸运。

We are born different. As long as we insist on chasing our dreams, we will be fortunate no matter where we go. Everyone will have his/her fortune. When we find it, we should embrace it. The moment that we harvest the gift brought by such fortune will be our most fortunate moment. In 2020, I felt fortunate to receive so much wealth on the path of chasing my dreams.

陈 浩
Tommy Chen

一枚九四年的北方小伙，在充满挑战的现实中奔跑的追梦人。平时少言但不呆板，内心世界丰富。热爱音乐、美食和旅行，向往洒脱的人生。能享受一个人的独处，也期待一群人的欢闹。立志年少有为，相信未来可期。

Tommy is a young man born in 1994 in north China and an unremitting dream chaser in the challenging reality. He speaks little yet is never rigid. This sentimental music, food and travelling enthusiast yearns for a free life. He enjoys the solitude of being alone and at the same time looks forward to the jollification of being with a bunch of people. Determined to achieve something at a young age, he believes in an amazing future.

佛系 + 奋斗 = 理想

A Buddha Mind + Struggling = Ideal

■ William Qiu

2020 年 3 月初的清晨，还有些许的寒意，在儿子的脑袋上亲了一口，收拾好行装，踏上了去机场的路。从北纬 31 度来到了北纬 21 度，开始了我的施璐德生涯。

佛系

加入施璐德前，就参与过智利锂电工厂项目，去环球大厦拜访过，也曾带施璐德同事一起参观过燕达工厂。早就听闻施璐德是业界的一朵"奇葩"，我有幸加入了这个"奇葩"大家庭，而今更直观真切地感受到一种以信任为基础的企业文化，给了员工更多自由的空间，没有特别的上下级关系，没有发展的天花板，大家互相尊重，真诚相待。

The early morning in March was still a bit cold. After giving a kiss on the head of my son, I packed my bags and headed for the airport. With a flight from the 31 degrees north latitude to 21 degrees north latitude, I started my career at CNOOD.

A Buddha Mind

Before joining CNOOD, I had participated in the lithium-ion battery factory project in Chile, visited the Universal Tower and brought CNOOD employees to Yanda Factory for a visit. I have long heard of the "oddness" of CNOOD in the industry. Now I have the honor to be part of this "odd" family, and I can more intuitively feel a corporate culture based on trust. Employees are given more room of freedom. There is no bureancratic relationship between superiors and subordinates and no development ceiling. We respect each other and treat each other sincerely.

缅甸泵站项目，是我参与的第一个海外一线项目。俗话说逆水行舟，不进则退，先是遭遇疫情封城封国，后又碰上了洪水，但是施璐德团队终于在 2021 年 1 月完成了泵站试车。Dennis 常说，一定要坚持做一件事，用 5 年、10 年坚持做下去，定然成为行业大咖。疫情没有吓倒我们，洪水没有冲垮我们，还有什么理由不坚持做下去呢？放下顾虑，往前冲！

The pump station project in Myanmar was my first overseas frontline project. There is a Chinese saying that he who does not advance loses ground. Despite lockdowns imposed because of COVID-19 and the subsequent flood hitting the region, the CNOOD team eventually completed the pump station trial run this January. Just as Dennis often says, we must persist in doing one thing for five years or ten years, we will certainly become an industry leader. The epidemic has not frightened us, and the flood has not washed us away. What's the reason for not doing it persistently? Cast aside the worries and forge ahead!

在项目遇到挫折的时候，常敦促自己慢下来，抛下杂念，整理头绪。佛系不是消极，也不是逃避，不是软弱，更不是颓废，它只是一种态度，佛系在一定程度上可以发掘自己的潜能，接受佛系，就是接受真实的自己。在无助孤独的时候，佛系也是一种不错的选项。

Whenever setbacks hit a project, I often urge myself to slow down, clear my head and organize my thoughts. A Buddha mind is not passivity, escape, weakness or decadence. It's an attitude which can tap your potentials to some extent. Accepting a Buddha mind is accepting your true self. A Buddha mind is a nice choice when you feel helpless and lonely.

奋斗的意义

395个日夜,外公在2020年4月11日的凌晨静静地走了,去吃他最爱的桂花年糕、酒酿圆子了。自中风后失语,外公再也没有说过一个字,我们只能相视无奈地苦笑。出发前的晚上,看着外公憔悴的面容,童年的回忆,三十年的光阴,闪现过脑海。我明白,此去可能是永别。再见了,外公!

《圣经》里说:"你必汗流满面才得糊口。"我们的工作一半是为了生存,一半是为了发展。生存是为了更好地发展,发展是为了更好地生存。人生的精彩在于奋斗的过程,并不在于结果。在施璐德这个公平自由的平台上,每个人都有机会创造属于自己的篇章,这个时代是属于奋斗者的时代。

用佛系调适心灵,用奋斗实现自我,那么理想肯定就在不远的前方。

The Significance of Struggling

After 395 days and nights since his stroke, my maternal Grandpa passed away quietly on the morning hours of April 11, 2020. He must have gone to eat his favourite osmanthus rice cakes and sweet sticky rice dumplings made with liquor. He hadn't spoken a word after the stroke, and we often looked at each other and smiled bitterly. On the night before my departure, I went to see him. When I looked at his haggard face, my childhood memories and the past thirty years of life crossed my mind. I knew that this might be my last time seeing him! Goodbye, Grandpa!

It is written in the Bible: "In the sweat of thy face shalt thou eat bread." Our work is half for survival and half for development. Survival is for better development, and development for better survival. The brilliance of life lies in the process of struggle, not in the result. On this fair and free platform of CNOOD, everyone has the opportunity to create his own chapter. This is an era for the strivers.

Soothe your heart with a Buddha mind, and realize your self-worth with struggle. Then the ideal must be not far ahead.

无题

Untitled

■ Heron Tang

疫情重兮施援手
众心一兮路复明
志不懈兮德为本
创新绩兮成砚铭

  Help with the fight against the severe epidemic;

  Work together to take a bright path;

  Make unremitting efforts and put virtue first;

  Score innovation achievements and build a good reputation.

2020 塞拉利昂行

A Trip to Sierra Leone in 2020

■ Charles Lee

2020年1月4日，经过周密的前期准备，我们一行5人，从上海启程，前往西非小国塞拉利昂开展为期10天的商务考察。沿途目之所及，耳之所闻，颇多感触。

塞拉利昂，是联合国公布的世界最不发达国家之一，其人类发展指数曾连续数年排名世界末位。出发之前，我对这个轮廓像一颗钻石、面积只有7.1万平方千米的西非小国的全部印象，只停留在电影《血钻》的镜头里。也因《血钻》，很多人都知道这个国家盛产钻石。根据勘探数据，这个人口只有750万的国家，至少三分之一的国土下埋藏着钻石，钻石储量超过2 300万克拉，可谓遍地钻石。就常理而言，这样的国家理应因钻石而兴，百姓安居乐业，社会井然有序。但出现在我们眼前的真实的塞拉利昂，却是一个破败不堪、民生凋敝、被上帝遗忘的国度。当地人称钻石为被诅咒了的资源，对普通百姓而言，钻石带来的不是财富与安宁，而是战争、贫穷、甚至死亡。

After meticulous preparations, the five of us set out from Shanghai on January 4, 2020 and started a 10-day business trip to a small West African country Sierra Leone. I was quite emotionally stirred by what I saw and heard along the journey.

Sierra Leone is one of the least developed countries in the world released by the United Nations, and has the lowest human development index in the world for several years. Before our trip, my impression on this small West African country shaped like a diamond and having an area of about 71,000 square kilometers was limited to the shots in the movie *Blood Diamond*. Because of the movie, many come to know that it's a country rich in diamonds. According to the exploration data, at least a third of the land of this country of 7.5 million people is covered in diamonds. The diamond reserves of Sierra Leone exceed 23 million carats. It can be said that diamonds are everywhere

塞拉利昂这片土地上人类活动的最早踪迹，依据现有史料可上溯至 2 500 年前，当时有 Bulom 人、Sherbo 人、Loko 人、Susu 人、Fula 以及 Limba 人在此居住。曼迪人于 13 世纪进入该地区。1462 年，葡萄牙殖民主义者侵入，荷兰、法国和英国殖民者亦随后运来 400 名"自由"黑奴，定居弗里敦（即自由城）。塞拉利昂因葡萄牙航海家探险家 Pedro de Sintra 而得名，他在公元 1462 年在西非海岸航行时似乎受到了该国山脉的启发，用葡语将其称为 Serra Leoa，直接意思是狮子山。而弗里敦处处此起彼伏的山丘，也印证了这个说法。山丘连绵不接，海拔都在 200 米以内。葡萄牙人在这片土地上的踪迹，随着 17 世纪大英帝国的崛起，而告没落。当时的塞拉利昂，是非洲成千上万的黑奴被贩往北美与西印度的集散中心。这段历史，可以在现在 Bunce Island 的商贸港，以及弗里敦的博物馆里窥得。

in this country. As far as common sense is concerned, such country should have prospered because of diamonds and maintained a good social order, where people live and work in peace and contentment. However, we are looking at a broken and desolated country forgotten by God. The locals consider diamonds a cursed resource. For ordinary people, what diamonds have brought are not fortune and peace, but warfare, poverty or even death.

The earliest traces of human activity on this land date back to 2500 years ago according to existing historical data. Bulom, Sherbo, Loko, Susu, Fula and Limba Peoples once lived here. Mandy People entered this region in the 13th century. In 1462, the Portuguese colonialists invaded this region. The Dutch, French and British colonists later brought 400 "free" slaves and settled in Freetown. Sierra Leone is named after Portuguese navigator and explorer Pedro de Sintra. When he sailed off the coast of West Africa in 1462, he seemed to be inspired by the mountains of this region and called it Serra Leoa in Portuguese, meaning the Mountain of Lion. Freetown is located amid the undulating hills less than 200 meters above sea level, which confirms this tale. The traces of the Portuguese on this land disappeared as the British Empire rose in the 17th century. Sierra Leone was then a distribution center for thousands of slaves from Africa to North America and the West Indies. This history can be found

18世纪，随着蓄奴制的土崩瓦解，以及英国觉醒人士的呼吁，塞拉利昂被选为重获自由的非洲黑奴新的家园。而今弗里敦市中心古老的木棉树，见证了那段不堪回首的岁月，从世界各地释放的黑奴，被有序地送往塞拉利昂。随着20世纪60年代席卷非洲大陆的殖民地自治运动的开展，塞拉利昂最终在1961年独立，然而，这个多灾多难的国家，没有经历和平与发展。在独立后，随之而来的却是多年的权利斗争以及一系列的军事政变，并最终在1991年彻底失控，演化为全面内战，这场内战带给这个国家的创伤至今难以愈合，在大街上，随处可见肢体残缺的中年人，他们表情木讷，神情低沉。到2002年内战结束，共造成5万多人死亡，200万人流离失所，内战结束了，但是留下了10万多肢体残缺的人。和平终现曙光，然而对普通百姓而言一切似乎来得太晚太晚。英国有句谚语：战争一开打，地狱便打开。而地狱的大门，似乎到现在还未完全关上。

除钻石以外，塞拉利昂还拥有铝矾土1.22亿吨，金红石1亿吨，铁矿石2亿

at the commercial port on the present-day Bunce Island, and at the museum in Freetown.

With the collapse of slavery and the appeal of awakening Britons, Sierra Leone was chosen as the new home for freed African slaves in the 18th century. The ancient kapok trees in the heart of Freetown bear witness to that terrible time when the slaves freed all over the world were orderly sent back to Sierra Leone. Following the colonial autonomy movement that swept the African continent in the 1960s, Sierra Leone finally gained independence in 1961. However, this troubled country had no peace or development. Independence was followed by years of power struggles and a series of military coups. The situation finally lost control in 1991 and a full-scale civil war broke out. This civil war inflicted wounds on the country that are still hard to heal today. Middle-aged low-spirited men with broken limbs and stiff expressions can be frequently seen on the streets. It was not until 2002 that the civil war was ended. It resulted in about 50,000 deaths, 2 million people displaced and 100,000 people physically disabled. Peace was at last dawning. For ordinary people, however, everything seemed to be too late. There is a British proverb going that when war begins, then hell openeth. It seems that the gate of the hell has not been completely closed yet.

In addition to diamonds, Sierra Leone boasts 122 million tons of bauxite,

吨。此外，大西洋边上485千米的海岸线，以及年平均温度27℃的热带季风气候为塞拉利昂提供了丰富的邦加鱼、金枪鱼、黄花鱼、青鱼和大虾等水产资源。囿于社会整体发展水平滞后，缺乏现代化的捕捞工具，海洋资源不能充分利用。

2018年，军人出身、信奉天主教的马达·比奥总统执政，随之在塞拉利昂历史上破天荒第一次提出并推行义务教育。太久的失落，终将迎来希望的曙光，但愿在新的政府的带领下，这个饱经沧桑与苦难的国家能够一步步走上正轨，使百姓安居乐业。期待这个大西洋边上的钻石王国发出越来越耀眼的光芒。那颗躺在大英博物馆里的1 000克拉的"塞拉里昂之星"将见证和平、文明曙光的来临。我们也将与塞拉利昂人民一道，为国家发展、民生改善做出持续努力。

100 million tons of rutile and 200 million tons of iron ore. Furthermore, the 485-kilometer coastline of the Atlantic Ocean and the tropical monsoon climate with an average annual temperature of 27℃ provide Sierra Leone with abundant fish resources such as bonga, tuna, yellow croaker, herring and prawn. Limited by the backward development of the whole society and the lack of modern fishing tools, the marine resources cannot be fully utilized.

In 2018, President Mada Bio, a soldier and Catholic, came into power. And for the first time in the history of Sierra Leone, commission and compulsory education were introduced. After such a long period of loss, hope has finally dawned. It's hoped that under the leadership of the new government, this country which has suffered so much will be able to steer itself on the right track and help its people to live and work in peace. Let's look forward to this diamond kingdom on the coast of the Atlantic Ocean shining brighter and brighter. The 1,000-carat Star of Sierra Leone lying in the British Museum will bear witness to the dawn of peace and civilization. We will also work with the Sierra Leonean people to make sustained efforts for national development and improvement of people's livelihood.

Lungi 机场（塞拉利昂全国唯一机场）去往首都弗里敦的跨海快艇（凌晨两点）
The Sea-crossing Speed Boat of Lungi Airport (The Only Airport of Sierra Leone) Heading toward the capital Freetown at 2:00 a.m.

天真的孩童，忧伤的面容
The Sad Faces of the Innocent Children

山丘鸟瞰，雾气朦胧不远处即大西洋
A Bird's-eye View on the Hill in the Fog and the Atlantic Ocean in the Near Distance

跨大西洋渡轮一瞥
A Glimpse of the Transatlantic Ferry

街头掠影
A Snapshot of the Street

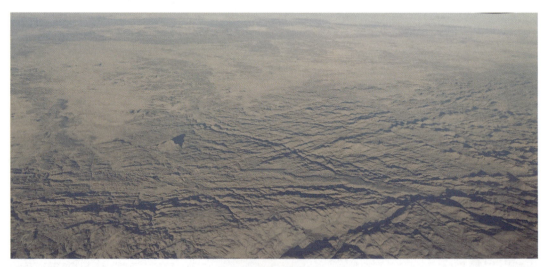

归途中的撒哈拉沙漠
The Sahara Desert on Our Homeward Journey

李 鹏
Charles Lee

中共党员，山西忻州人，2014年毕业于上海对外经贸大学，翻译硕士，同年加入施璐德，主要从事市场开发工作。

Member of the Communist Party of China, born in Xinzhou, Shanxi Province, 2014 graduate of Shanghai University of International Business and Economics with a master's degree in translation. After graduation, he joined CNOOD, mainly engaged in market development.

时代的浪潮与个人选择

The Tide of the Times and Personal Choice

■ Raven Song

2020年的关键词有新冠肺炎疫情、居家办公、中美博弈、武汉加油、疫苗……

突如其来的疫情打乱了世界正常运行的轨迹，使国际政治和经济发生了巨变。如今中国成为了经济全球化的捍卫者，而美国却成为贸易保护主义的先锋。2020年好似一条分界线，注定成为不平凡。

同时，特殊的一年也给了自己更多的时间去思考，似乎明白了一个道理：在时代的浪潮里，个人的选择是如此重要。

回顾历史，只有顺时代潮流而拼搏向上的人生，才足以在波澜壮阔的历史长河中永载史册。在不同的时代，踏准时代的潮流，在对的方向上做出正确选择、努力奋斗，这是实现人生目标的必要条件。我

Keywords in 2020 have been COVID-19, homeworking, China-U.S. game, Wuhan fighting, vaccine ...

The sudden outbreak of COVID-19 has disrupted the normal course of the world and brought about profound changes in international politics and economics. China has now become the champion of economic globalization while the U.S. has become the vanguard of trade protectionism. The year 2020 is like a dividing line, destined to become extraordinary.

Meanwhile, such an eventful year has given me more time to think, and I seem to have grasped a truth that personal choice is very important tn the tide of the times.

A review on history reveals that only a life pushing upward along with the trend of the times can be immortalized in history. Going along with the trend of the times in different eras, making the right

党的革命先驱、共和国建设者、改革开放先锋、互联网科技巨头创始人，这一批奋斗者正是乘时代而起，顺时代而昌。

所以，每一个人做出人生重大选择之前，有必需考虑是否是顺势而为，而非逆流而上。

毫无疑问，公司的发展规划和个人的职业选择都需要符合时代发展潮流的大方向上。2020年，公司正式发布了《施璐德十年发展纲领（2020—2029）》，其中重点提出了未来的战略定位和十年规划目标："未来十年，坚持以工程版块为龙头，以工程创造的贸易为基础，以教育为支撑的发展战略""持续拓展全球布局""大力拓展业务领域""不断延伸产业链"等。该纲领正是正确站在了时代主题的大方向上做出的发展指引。

在百年未有之大变局的格局下，我有如下思考。

choices and working on them are the requirements for achieving your goals in life. The revolutionary pioneers of the Communist Party of China, the builders of the People's Republic of China, those who became rich first in the opening-up and reform and internet technology giants ... all these strivers have rode and prospered with the times.

So before you make the big choices in life, it's important to consider whether you are going with the trend or against it.

There is no doubt that a conpany's development planning and personal career choices need to be made in accordance with the general direction of the development trend of the times. In 2020, CNOOD released *Ten-year Development Guideline of CNOOD (2020–2029)*. The future strategic positioning and ten-year planning goals are put forward: "In the next ten years, CNOOD will lead by the engineering segment and insist on the education-supported development strategy based on trade created by engineering," "expand the global presence on an ongoing basis," "vigorously expand into new businesses" and "continuously extend the industry chain." The guideline is a development guideline developed in the general direction of the theme of the times.

Personally, I have the following thoughts from the perspective of the theme of the times of profound change unseen in a century:

1. 世界之大，亦有广阔天地

欧美等西方国家，主导了近代以来的以蒸汽机、电气化、计算机为代表的工业革命，进而主导了世界的格局和发展。近年来，随着中国等一批发展中国家的崛起，一部分发展中国家和地区也已经开展现代化建设。但是，我们要看到，世界范围内的发展力亟待解放，世界现代化建设方兴未艾，大部分人还没有过上"好日子"，集中体现在非洲和部分东南亚国家，这些是公司重点布局的区域，也是个人选择的重点方向。

2. 中国模式的推广之路

推广中国模式从来不是简单复制，需要因地制宜一步步实施。比如，中国帮助非洲国家建设了大量的基础设施；中国在部分东南亚国家投资合作建厂，帮助其建立初步的工业制造业基础，解决就业问题。这种密切合作、深度合作、携手并进的模式才是良性的、可持续的。

1. There is vast space in the big world

Western countries in Europe and North America have led the industrial revolutions represented by steam engine, electrification and computer since modern times and then dominated the pattern and development of the world. With the rise of a group of developing countries such as China in recent years, some people in developing countries and regions have stepped into modern life. However, we must recognize that worldwide development forces need to be unleashed and the global modernization drive is still advancing. Most of the people are yet to lead a "good life," which is reflected in Africa and some Southeast Asian countries. They are the key areas in the layout of corporate development and the important direction of personal choice.

2. The promotion of the China model

Promoting the China model is never simple duplication and needs to be implemented step by step according to local conditions. For instance, China has helped Africa build a lot of infrastructure. China has invested and built factories in some Southeast Asian countries to help them build a preliminary industrial manufacturing foundation and solve employment problems. Such a model of close, in-depth and hand-in-hand cooperation is a sound and sustainable one.

3. 讲好中国故事

作为致力于海外工程的中国企业，需要重视和维护中国在海外的良好形象。当前，即使资讯发达，但是相当多的国家普通民众对中国还有颇多的误解和负面的评价，其中的原因非常复杂，但总体上存在一个规律，即中美在各国的接受程度上是处于零和状态的。以东南亚为例，泰国、马来西亚、柬埔寨等对中国文化的认同度较高，对美国的认同度相对低；菲律宾、新加坡、印度尼西亚等国对中国的认同度较低，而对美国认同度相对高。我们首先需要正确认识这个客观事实，也要做出一些举措去改善和维护中国的海外形象，如提升中国消费品牌形象、善用社交媒体渠道、加强公共外交举措、促进民间组织交流等。这样我们可以逐步提升国家和自身的信用，要知道，好的信用需要几代人数十年的努力积累，但毁掉它只需要一个蠢货做一件蠢事就够了。所以做好海外工程，需要我们重视在海外的形象，讲好中国故事，让世界读懂中国，让世界人民真正意识到中国是营造良好未来发展空间的国家。

3. Tell a good story about China

Chinese enterprises committed to overseas projects need to pay attention to and maintain a good image of China overseas. Despite the advanced information nowadays, there are still quite a lot of misunderstandings and negative comments about China by the general public in many countries. The reasons are very complicated, but there is a general pattern that China and the U.S. are in a zero-sum state in terms of the acceptance degree of other countries. Taking Southeast Asia for example, Thailand, Malaysia, Cambodia and other countries have a high degree of acceptance of China, but a relatively low degree of acceptance of the U.S.; in the Philippines, Singapore, Indonesia and other countries, the degree of acceptance of China is low, but the degree of acceptance of the U.S. is relatively high. We need to have a correct understanding of this objective fact and also take some measures to improve and maintain China's image overseas, such as enhancing the image of Chinese consumer brands, making good use of social media channels, strengthening public diplomacy measures, and promoting exchanges among non-governmental organizations. In this way we can gradually improve the credit of our country and our own. As we know, good credit takes generations and decades to build, but it only takes one fool to do something stupid to destroy it. To execute overseas projects well, therefore, we

全球正处百年未有之大变局。对个人而言，需要站在此历史大方向上对未来做出重要的抉择。国家、个人的发展，从来不是要成为谁，而是成为更好的自己。

need to pay attention to the image of China overseas, tell a good story about China, let the world understand China, and let people around the world truly realize that China is a country that creates a good space for future development.

In response to the profound change unseen in a century, for individuals, it is in this historical context that important decisions need to be made about the future. The development of a country or an individual is never about who you are, but about becoming a better you.

宋瑞文
Raven Song

中国石油大学（北京）硕士，2018年6月加入施璐德。
坚信：未来三十年，做多中国，做多自己！

Raven, graduate of China University of Petroleum with a master's degree, joined CNOOD in June 2018. He is a firm believer of going along with China and with himself in the next 30 years!

因为有梦，所以远方

Head toward the Distance for the Pursuit of the Dream

■ Jodie Zhou

1. 初相识

最开始，我是通过公司公众号和以往的年鉴来了解施璐德的。在阅读公众号和年鉴时，我不禁对施璐德充满了好奇，好奇这家公司到底有着怎样的魔力，仅仅是文字描述就让人感到如此的温暖。

2020年的7月，我正式地开始了与CNOOD的初相识。

在踏入施璐德的第一天，我就迎来了实习的第一个任务——处理一份有关世界银行的文件。在最初的文件阅读中，我虽然基于Fay对该份文件的整理要求进行了处理，但是却习惯性地忽略了词条介绍和附录，仅仅整理了自己认为重要的内容。在Danni检查我所整理的内容时，我在文件阅读上广度和深度的欠缺暴露无遗。这让我深刻感受到，在阅读一份文件时，切忌先入为主，只有在完全熟知后，才能分辨出重要和相对不重要的部分。之后，在给世行回复的邮件中，基于Fay总结的几个要点和Danni的修改意见，我顺利完成

1. Meeting with CNOOD

I first came to know about CNOOD through its official account and previous yearbooks. As I read about the heart-warming articles, I couldn't help but wonder what magic power this Company has.

In July 2020, I officially met with CNOOD.

On my first day as an intern at CNOOD, I was assigned with my first task—processing a World Bank document. Although I sorted out the document as required by Fay, I habitually forgot about entry introductions and appendixes and only summarized the contents I thought important. My lack of breadth and depth in document reading was thoroughly exposed when Danni reviewed my document summary. It made me realize that it's not wise to read documents with prior hypothesis bias

了邮件回复的内容。由此，算是给自己的第一个实习任务交上了答卷。

在这之后，我组织过会议，了解了组织会议的一般流程；旁听过商务会谈，见识了精彩的商业对话；处理过工作文件，深刻认识了复核的重要性。同时，我也逐渐熟悉了这个温暖的地方。在这里，你会发现，所有高层与员工都是坐在一起办公，开放式办公模式提升了整个办公环境的活力和员工的激情，充分彰显了施璐德的核心文化——共创、共治、共享；在这里，你会发现，相较于将施璐德简单定义为"公司"，"大家庭"似乎更为合适，每一个施璐德人在CNOOD这个大家庭里相互关心、创造开心！

and it's important to fully understand them before differentiating the important parts from the less important parts. With the key points summarized by Fay and the revisions of Danni, I successfully replied the email and completed my first task as an intern.

After that, I organized meetings and familiarized myself with the general flow of meeting organization; I sat on business talks and heard wonderful business dialogues; in the processing of work documents, I came to realize the importance of double-checking. I also gradually got to know this heart-warming place. Here you will find all executives and employees sitting in the same open office, which enhances the vitality of the office environment and the passion of employees and manifests CNOOD's core culture — co-creation, co-governance and sharing; here you will find that CNOOD is more of a big family than a company where every member cares about each other and creates happiness!

2. 渐相知

继短暂的 7 月份实习之后，我在 2020 年 10 月 13 号这一天再次踏入越商大厦 8 楼。所有的相遇，都是久别的重逢，而这一次将是我与施璐德的第二次相遇。

（1）参与资格预审（prequalification）的准备。

为了给新人提供学习机会，Fay 特意让 2020 年公司的几个新同事参与了一个阿尔及利亚项目的 PQ 准备环节。在参与过程中，Fay 指导着我们开展 PQ 的准备工作，如了解该项目的背景和业主的相关信息、根据了解到的信息初步判断该项目的可行性、以该项目的背景和要求为导向有针对性地填写 PQ 的相关内容。此次工作让我了解到一个较为完整的 PQ 所包含的内容，也体会到完成一个项目的不易。工程项目从投标、中标到项目执行，整个周期长达数月，是一场持久战，更是一门学问。在项目里，各团队成员分工明确，相互配合，同舟共济，充分彰显团队合作的魅力。

（2）参与编撰员工手册。

在与公司同事逐渐熟络之时，非常有幸能与韩总、Danni、Heather 和 Loreen 一起编撰新版的员工手册。在将前一版的

2. Gradually knowing CNOOD

After my short internship in July, I set foot on the 8th floor of Yueshang Plaza again on October 13. All encounters are reunions after a long separation. This would be my second encounter with CNOOD.

(1) Preparation for PQ.

To provide opportunities for newcomers, Fay assigned the several new recruits of the company this year to prepare for PQ of the Algeria Project. Fay guided us on how to unfold PQ preparations, including learning about the project background and client information, making a preliminary judgement on the feasibility of the project according to the information learned, and filling in the PQ oriented towards the project background and requirements. This job allowed me to understand the contents of a relatively complete PQ and see the difficulties before a project can be completed. From bidding, bid winning and project execution, an engineering project has a cycle of several months. It's a protracted war and more importantly, a science. All team members in the project have clear division of labor, cooperate with each other and work together, fully demonstrating the charm of team cooperation.

(2) Formulation of Employee Handbook.

As I became to know the co-workers better, I was honored to be part of the formulation team of the new Employee

员工手册进行翻译之后，我也从新同事的视角针对此次编撰提出了自己的看法。在一个多月的时间里，每周四的小会议室总会被我们编辑小团队征用。在每周数小时的讨论中，我们各抒己见，员工手册在思维碰撞的火花中逐渐完善。在此次的编撰机会中，我深悉了公司的架构、文化以及相关制度。同时，我也充分感受到团队合作的氛围，学习到同事们的行政思维，更加敬佩施璐德的社会担当。"老池的愿望就是建一所希望小学，鼓励施璐德人去支教""老池还想建一所施璐德养老院呢"，Dennis 的每一个愿望都与生意无关，但却让施璐德的脊梁更加高挺。

Handbook together with Mr. HAN, Danni, Heather and Loreen. After translating the previous Employee Handbook, I shared my views from the perspective of a new employee. For about a month, the small conference room would be occupied by us editing team every Thursday. During hours of discussion, we each expressed our views, and the Employee Handbook was improved with the sparks of thoughts. This opportunity allowed me to gain an in-depth understanding on the architecture, culture and relevant regulations of the company and feel the atmosphere of team cooperation. While learning about the administrative mindset of the co-workers, I admired the sense of social responsibility of CNOOD even more. "Dennis wants to build a Project Hope primary school and encourages the employees of CNOOD to work as volunteer teachers." "Dennis also wants to build a CNOOD Elderly Home." Each wish of Dennis is not related to business and yet makes CNOOD stand up straighter.

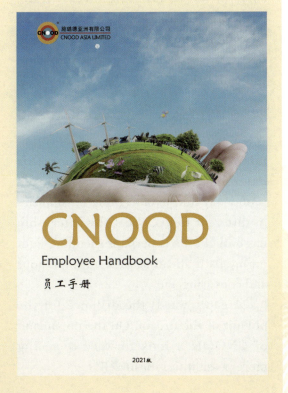

（3）参与注册子公司。

在着手西班牙子公司注册的相关事宜时，我主要负责POA公证和NIE申请，其间一直与香港公司的Pat积极沟通。从最开始的一筹莫展，到逐渐对公司注册的流程有了大致了解，其中有自我的成长，也有来自同事的帮助。此次公司注册过程中令我印象最深刻的是时差问题。在与西班牙驻上海总领事馆进行邮件沟通、在询问公司西班牙律师意见的过程中，时差问题使公司注册的整体速度变得很慢。作为一家国际公司，有效地解决时差问题、提高工作效率、对邮件快速反应是非常重要的，这也是我需要继续学习和总结的地方。

3. 盼相惜

施璐德所需要的是全面型人才，是全面发展的员工，此次实习让我实现了全方位进步，探索了自己在各个工作领域的可能。若要说这次实习给我带来了什么，那或许是：让我在浮躁、迷茫的年纪看清了前行的路。

因为有梦，所以远方。在施璐德这片梦想之地上，我期待着看到实现更多可能的自己！

(3) Company registration.

Before handling the registration of our Spanish subsidiary, I was mainly responsible for notarization of POA and application for NIE and had been actively communicating with Pat from our Hong Kong subsidiary. As I gradually gained a rough idea of company registration process, I grew and received assistance from the co-workers. What this task impressed me most was the time difference. During my communication with the Consulate General of Spain in Shanghai via email and inquiry of the legal opinions of our Spanish attorneys, time difference slowed down the process of company registration. It is highly important for an international corporation to effectively resolve the time difference issue, enhance work efficiency and quickly respond to emails. It's also a focus of my further study and summarization.

3. Valuing CNOOD

What CNOOD needs are all-round talent and employees. Through this internship, I have made progress in an all-round way and explored my possibilities in different fields. What this internship has brought me is perhaps shedding light on my path ahead at such an impetuous and confusing age.

Head towards the distance for the pursuit of the dream. On the dreamland of CNOOD, I look forward to seeing more possibilities for myself!

周 颖
Jodie Zhou

中南财经政法大学金融硕士，一个地道的、无辣不欢的湖北人，一个捕获到美食便能开心一天的金牛座。虽然目前"涉世未深"，但时刻相信生活充满可能，并一直保持着乐观、开朗的态度面对工作和生活！

With a master's degree in finance from Zhongnan University of Economics and Law, she is an authentic Hubei native who is crazy for spicy food. She is a Taurus who can have a happy day after a delicious meal. Although currently "inexperienced," she always believes that life is full of possibilities and has always maintained an optimistic, cheerful attitude towards work and life!

实 习 感 想

Thoughts after My Internship

■ Yingyue Cui

在过去的几个月里，我有幸作为一名远程实习生，参与了 CNOOD 技术部的日常工作。由于大学课程大多注重理论与数据结构而非项目实践，我非常庆幸能获得这样一个能将学到的知识应用于实践的机会。在刚开始实习的时候，因为网页相关的编程经验较少，我在两位资深 IT 人员的指导下花了一些时间学习相关知识，然后上手项目。在这个过程中，我填补了自己在许多理论知识与现实应用之间的空白，也学习了许多现代网站开发会用到的技术与框架。

前几周的学习主要围绕前端语言、框架以及 JavaScript 展开。虽然我在开始实习前对 HTML 和 CSS 都有所了解，但我还没有接触过 Bootstrap 这种广泛使用的

Over the past few months, I had the honor to work as a remote intern for the Technology Department of CNOOD. It was indeed a wonderful opportunity to apply what's learned to reality as most undergraduate courses focus on theory and data structures rather than project practice. At the beginning of my internship, I spent some time under the mentoring of two senior IT technicians to learn relevant knowledge and get started with the project because I had little webpage related programming experience. This internship has allowed me to fill in a lot of gaps between theoretical knowledge and practical application, and I learned plenty of technologies and frameworks that can be used in modern website development.

The first few weeks of learning focused on front-end languages, frameworks and JavaScript. Despite some knowledge on HTML and CSS

排版插件。在学习 Bootstrap 时，我一开始只会阅读使用说明和观看教程，直到开始修改项目后才发现理论知识远远不足，所以我又自己建了一个页面，通过实验进一步熟悉操作方法。实习结束后，我在下一个项目中就独立使用 Bootstrap 制作了一个小程序的官网，这与我暑假期间学到的知识和获得的训练有着密不可分的联系。

第一阶段的任务结束后，我又开始学习网络爬虫技术。因为对 python 已经比较熟练，所以对这一内容的学习比较顺利。第一次实践时，两位老师看完我的结果，指导我辨别了网站设置的反爬虫机制，并且告诉我如何优化代码。这让我意识到许多技术在现实中应用时要注意细节，不可大意。

在实习过程中，两位老师给了我许多帮助，并且带领我了解了许多网页开发的基础知识和框架，为我后期的学习奠定了坚实的基础。他们自始至终都非常友好，让我从一开始的不太习惯提问题，只顾埋头苦干，到后来发现适时地提出困扰自己的问题能极大地提高效率。经过几个月的学习与训练，我深刻地意识到学校所教授的理论知识与现实应用之间的鸿沟，在接触了许多广泛使用的技术后，为自己

before I started my internship, I had not been exposed to Bootstrap, a widely used typesetting plug-in. When learning Bootstrap, I only read the instructions and watched the tutorials at first. It was not until I began to modify the project that I realized that the theoretical knowledge was far from sufficient. Hence, I set up a page by myself to further familiarize myself with the operation method through experiments. After the internship, I independently made a small program's official website with Bootstrap in my next project, which was closely related to the knowledge I learned and training I received during the summer vacation.

After the first phase of the task was accomplished, I began to learn web crawler technology. My familiarity with python gave me no challenge in learning it. In my first practice, two teachers read my results, instructed me to identify the anti-crawler mechanism set by the website and told me how to optimize the codes. This made me realize that the application of many technologies in reality requires attention to details and constant caution.

During the internship, the two teachers gave me a lot of help and introduced me to a lot of basic knowledge and frameworks of web development, which has laid a solid foundation for my later study. Their friendliness has allowed me to change from a hard worker not used to asking questions to an efficient worker asking questions in the right time. After several months of study and training, I was deeply aware of

以后的学习确定了方向。两位老师对我写的代码的修改，也让我更加注重计算机工作中严格的标准和严谨的态度，促使我每次写完程序后进行检查和优化，尽量使自己的代码干净整洁，易于理解。非常感谢CNOOD给我这次机会，能够近距离接触企业级软件技术，并且能够跟从业内专业人士学习应用型编程。

the gap between theoretical knowledge taught in school and practical application, and I was exposed to many widely used technologies, which help define my future research interests. The code revisions made by the two teachers have allowed me to develop a more rigorous standard and a more prudent attitude in computer, reviewing and optimizing the codes to keep them neat and comprehensible. I am grateful to CNOOD for giving me this opportunity to get close to enterprise-level software technology and learn applied programming from professionals in the industry.

崔颖月
Yingyue Cui

康奈尔大学计算机科学专业大二在读学生，毕业后有意向进入软件开发领域。闲暇时间里喜欢写作、烘焙、做翻译、看脱口秀。在大一的暑假期间，有幸在施璐德完成自己的第一份实习，了解了许多计算机领域的专业知识与行业标准。

Now a sophomore in computer science at Cornell University, I envision myself working in software development after my graduation. In my spare time, I like writing, baking, translating and watching talk shows. I was honored to have my first internship at CNOOD during the summer vacation of my freshman year, and I have learned a lot of professional knowledge and industry standards in computer science.

实 习 感 想

Thoughts after My Internship

■ Yulan Liang

"正因为知识都是局部的，局部以外的部分才会变得分外迷人。我们才会想，剩下的部分是什么呢？这就为进一步探索留下了空间。而这个探索的空间，就是思维发展的空间，也是自我发展的空间。"作为一个从小就在校园里摸爬滚打的孩子，一直都对校园外的世界充满好奇。这一次，非常感谢施璐德给我宝贵的实习机会，在上海、扬中的两个多月里，我收获了一段美好又充实的回忆。

对公司整体的初印象

刚进公司的时候，我惊叹于公司关于时间安排的灵活性，但直到两个多月后的今天，才明白"项目团队是公司有机组成"的具体意思。让每个人都做公司的主人，是我从没有见过的经营模式：每一个人都是站在创业者的角度去思考问题，处

"It's because knowledge is local that the part beyond the locality is so charming. For this, we can't help but wonder what the remaining part is. This gives space for further exploration. This exploration space is the thinking development space as well as self-development space." Studying in school for such a long time, I have always been curious about the world outside school. Therefore, I am grateful for this valuable internship opportunity. The two odd months in Shanghai and Yangzhong have left me wonderful and fulfilling memories.

My First Impression of the Company

When I first joined the company, I was amazed at the flexibility in time arrangement. It's not until today after two months that I finally understand the meaning of the principle that "project teams are an integral part of the company."

理事情，在这里每个人都是平等的；CEO 和大家同坐在一起办公，公司鼓励支持员工去继续读书学习，办公室有一面书柜等……

了解了这些深入到细节的文化氛围和管理模式，再去看公司宏伟的战略目标——"不断延伸产业链向 EPC+ 方向发展"的时候，便觉得只要大家共同努力，一切皆有可能。这样积极向上的一种氛围里，每个人都有实现自我价值的机会，一定会吸引更多的人才加入。

It's a business model that I have never seen, where everyone serves as master of the company: every member of the staff thinks and deals with matters from a perspective of an entrepreneur on an equal footing; the CEO works in the same office area with the staff; the staff are encouraged to pursue further study; bookshelves are put up in the office...

After learning the corporate culture and management model in such details, I believe that everything is possible with concerted efforts, even for the ambitious strategic goal — extending the industry chain continuously to EPC+. Such an upbeat cultural atmosphere in which everyone has the freedom to fulfill self-worth will surely make the company a magnet for talented members.

在扬中：不一样的生活

感谢 Danni 的安排，我非常幸运能有机会去到现场，直接参与项目。在智利的喂鱼船项目的一个多月时间里，我跟随 Billy、Sherry 在工厂一起做项目管理。这段时间，我除去同 Sherry 一起去拍照片做日报之外，还参与了捐赠物资的准备以及最后物流阶段的各种准备工作和监督管理。

在扬中的生活，让我看到了更多的生活可能。

那里的村庄富有而静谧，每家的房子都是自己建造的别墅，特色鲜明；集市定时开门，有的饭馆周末不营业；居民不爱出门，上完班都回到家里。想到 2018 年的暑假，我前往康科德的瓦尔登湖，第一次惊叹国外的乡村、从小阅读的名著里的村庄，是那般安静和富饶，美得像一幅油画。当时，我多希望不久的将来，中国的乡村也可以像那样。2020 年的这段旅程，让我欣喜地看到，同样美丽的蓝天，极具特色的建筑，就在扬中的小镇里。

和我生长的环境不同，这一带的人都是从商世家。扬中长江一桥是一座由民间集资建造的大桥，它不仅仅结束了扬中

Yangzhong: A Different Life

Thanks to the arrangement of Danni, I was fortunate to have the opportunity to go to the site and be directly involved in the project. For about a month in the Chile-based fish feeding boat project, I worked with Billy and Sherry on project management in the factory. In addition to taking photos and preparing daily reports with Sherry, I participated in the preparation of donated materials and the preparation, supervision and management of the latter logistics stages.

My time in Yangzhong has allowed me to see more possibilities of living.

The villages there are rich and quiet, and each house is a self-built villa and highly personal; the market is open at regular hours, and some restaurants are closed on weekends; people don't like going out and go home after a day's work. In the summer of 2018, I went to Walden Pond in Concord and for the first time was amazed by the tranquility, richness and oil painting-like beauty of foreign countryside and villages written in the masterpieces I have read since my childhood. How I wished the countryside in China could be like this in the near future! The journey in 2020 brought me the delight to see the same beautiful blue sky and characteristic buildings in a small town of Yangzhong.

Different from the environment in which I grew up, this area is full of families with a long business history.

岛和外界无联通的历史，更承载着扬中人的梦想。疫情暴发期间，这里的人民开始投身于熔喷布的制造，或赚了一笔，或亏了许多。不管结果如何，他们都还再继续寻找新的商机并不断地尝试。听到这些勇敢拼搏的故事，让我心生敬畏，更启发着我，持续地尝试和创新是一辈子的事。

Yangzhong Yangtze River First Bridge is a bridge built with private funds, not only ending the history of Yangzhong Island's isolation from the outside world but also carrying the dream of Yangzhong people; during the outbreak of COVID-19, the locals were busy manufacturing melt-blown non-woven fabrics, some making a fortune and others suffering a huge loss. Regardless of the result, they continued to find new business opportunities and make new attempts. I stood in awe of these brave struggles and was inspired by the fact that constant experimentation and innovation is a lifetime effort.

在太仓润禾码头，我见到了许多形形色色的人。有的人习惯了在海上漂泊，到处奔走，没有办法在一个地方停留。我坐在码头看来来往往的船只，一层一层的浪花打来，听远方一艘船短鸣三声示意别的船只倒退，这种属于航海人特定的信号语言，突然莫名地让我有种归属感。生活在都市久了，感觉都快要丢失自己了。而这样亲近自然的自由好像是一种来自心底最原始的呼唤，让自己和自己的内心更加地亲近，焦躁的内心好像就有了归属的方向。

At Taicang Runhe Wharf, I saw different kinds of people. Some are used to drifting on the sea, running everywhere, reluctant to stay in a place. Sitting on the dock, I watched the ships coming and going and the waves hitting the shore and heard a ship in the distance making three short calls to signal the withdrawal of other ships. This signaling language unique to seafarers suddenly gave me a sense of belonging somehow. Living for such a long time in the city, I felt almost lost. The freedom to be close to nature seems to be the most primitive call from the bottom of my heart so that I can get closer to my inner self, and the restless heart seems to have found its place.

在上海的生活：学会关心世界

回到上海的这段时间，Danni让我制作 PPT 以便更细致地了解了公司的架构，我还去协助办理了营业执照变更，修改保密协议的模版，和同事一起做接待客人的准备工作和服务，并旁听了各种会议。这些经历让我了解到商务工作的具体内容，并见识到一些厉害的人物，他们谈话间的深层含义总是耐人寻味、令我受益匪浅。

傍晚的上海，许多人都会在公园里跑步健身；居民的投诉意识极强，每个人对自己和别人的权利都是尊重并加以保护的；这里的司机更加懂得礼让行人；很多大型的设计展览，许多全球不同的设计师买手店都会选择上海作为第一家旗舰店选址；最新的科技可以在这里体验到，广告牌都是学习新兴技术的好地方。上海的包容性和国际化体现在方方面面，在这样的一个城市里，你很难不想去听时事新闻，去了解这个世界正在发生什么。

Shanghai: Learning to Care about the World

Returning to Shanghai, Danni assigned me to create a PPT to gain a more thorough understanding of the corporate structure. I also assisted in the application for change in the business license, revised the template of confidentiality agreement, worked with others to prepare for and receive customers, and sat on various meetings. Such experience had shed light on the scope of business work and gave me the opportunity to meet amazing people who often speak in a thought-provoking manner, benefitting me a lot.

At dusk, many go jogging or work out in the parks; people have a strong awareness of complaint, and everyone respects and works to protect people's rights; drivers often yield to pedestrians; many large design exhibitions are held here, and many designer stores from all over the world choose Shanghai as the location for their first store in China; the latest technologies can be experienced here, and the advertising boards are wonderful places to learn emerging technologies. The inclusiveness and internationalization of Shanghai are embodied in every aspect. Living in such a city, you will be easily tempted to stay current with the news to learn about what is going on in the world.

未来可期

如果要问在施璐德实习的这段时间对我最大的改变是什么，那便是走在大街的盲人道上的时候，闭上眼睛我虽然还会感到害怕，但是我会开始告诉自己：相信自己脚上的感觉，我正在走向想到的那个地方。非常感谢在这里的每一位同事对我的照顾和教导，特别是 Danni、Sherry 还有 Billy 对我工作上的指导，还有 Nancy 和 Andy 愿意在疫情期间收留我。大家对我的帮助，让我对未来更加憧憬和笃定，希望大家都能在自己的人生道路上越走越精彩，希望施璐德能够越办越好，实现更大的业务范围和合作范围，在全球更多的角落留下我们中国的脚印。

A Promising Future

If you ask me what the biggest change my internship in CNOOD brought me is, I would say that I am still scared when walking on the blind sidewalks with eyes closed, yet I will start telling myself that trust what you feel in your feet as you are heading towards the direction you yearn for. I am truly grateful to all my colleagues here for their care and instruction, especially Danni, Sherry and Billy for their guidance on my work, and Nancy and Andy for taking me in during the epidemic. The assistance received has given me greater expectation and confidence in my future. Hopefully, all of you can make more and more wonderful progress in your life, and CNOOD can grow more, achieve a larger scope of business and cooperation, and leave the footprints of China in more corners of the world.

梁钰岚
Yulan Liang

硕士毕业于武汉大学物理学院，将要前往北京大学攻读激光加速器博士学位。非常喜欢旅游、交朋友，也特别幸运能在施璐德获得第一份实习，并收获了一段美好的回忆。

A fresh graduate from the School of Physics and Technology, Wuhan University and fond of tourism and making friends, I am fortunate to have my first internship at CNOOD and have obtained wonderful memories before my further study at Peking University for a doctoral degree in laser accelerator.

图书在版编目(CIP)数据

施璐德年鉴.2020:汉英对照/施璐德亚洲有限公司编.—上海:复旦大学出版社,2021.10
ISBN 978-7-309-15938-7

Ⅰ.①施… Ⅱ.①施… Ⅲ.①建筑企业-上海-2020-年鉴-汉、英 Ⅳ.①F426.9-54

中国版本图书馆 CIP 数据核字(2021)第 185122 号

施璐德年鉴.2020
SHILUDE NIANJIAN(2020)
施璐德亚洲有限公司　编
责任编辑/谢同君　李　荃

复旦大学出版社有限公司出版发行
上海市国权路 579 号　邮编:200433
网址:fupnet@fudanpress.com　http://www.fudanpress.com
门市零售:86-21-65102580　　团体订购:86-21-65104505
出版部电话:86-21-65642845
上海丽佳制版印刷有限公司

开本 787×1092　1/16　印张 8.75　字数 197 千
2021 年 10 月第 1 版第 1 次印刷

ISBN 978-7-309-15938-7/F·2832
定价:88.00 元

如有印装质量问题,请向复旦大学出版社有限公司出版部调换。
版权所有　侵权必究